D1355824

An Ordinary Murder

FOR RUTH

Lesley Moreland

An Ordinary Murder

AURUM PRESS

*Although this is a true story, the names
of some characters have been changed
to protect their identities.*

First published in Great Britain
2001 by Aurum Press Ltd
25 Bedford Avenue, London WC1B 3AT

A catalogue record for this book
is available from the British Library.

ISBN 1 85410 745 3

10 9 8 7 6 5 4 3 2 1
2005 2004 2003 2002 2001

Frontispiece photograph by Nigel Sorrell
from a video made by Laurence Gellor

Designed and typeset by Ken Wilson
Printed and bound in Great Britain by
MPG Books Ltd, Bodmin

Contents

Foreword

ONE OF THE MOST common journalistic clichés, often employed in the wake of a tragedy, is the suggestion that the victims are 'coming to terms with' their loss. How often have we heard the phrase used by a television reporter or read it in a newspaper account of an air crash, a drowning or a murder. But how do people 'come to terms with' the sudden death of a child, a partner or a close friend, particularly one whose life was just beginning and was full of promise?

During more than twenty years of covering crime, I have met many relations of murder victims. Some were eaten away by their pain in an almost tangible way. The father of one murdered girl said that he was only remaining alive in order to be able to kill his daughter's killer when he was finally released from prison. Another parent I met sought vengeance from anyone, however remotely connected with the killer, for their sins of negligence or indifference. Many were angry at the way they had been treated in the aftermath of murder, whether by a tactless detective, an insensitive journalist or a thoughtless court official. All were forever changed by an event which, however rare it might be in the United Kingdom, creates ripples that affect hundreds of relatives, friends and workmates of the victim and often strangers, who are touched by a cruel and pitiless killing.

At a meeting organised by the National Association for the Care and Resettlement of Offenders in London a few years ago, I was taking part in a discussion on the issue of crime and the media. By far the most interesting contribution to the debate came not from the platform but from a member of the audience who gave a vivid account of her own experience as the mother of a murder victim. She recounted how she had determined to meet the man responsible for her daughter's death, no matter how hard that journey would be and how long it would take.

I met Lesley Moreland again soon afterwards and was greatly impressed by her honesty and her desire, if not to 'come to terms with' her daughter Ruth's death, to at least try and harness her grief in a way that would allow her to live her life in the fashion that Ruth would have wanted, rather than being consumed by anger and bitterness.

Now she has written her own account of that long, hard battle to fight through her natural feelings of revulsion and revenge. At the same time she has explored society's attitude to punishment and redemption and the whole way in which we react to sudden tragedy. She has managed to do so in a way that is both accessible and moving, taking her evidence from both sides of the Atlantic as she examines our ways of dealing with murder.

Anyone who has ever been touched by a savage crime or who has wondered what effect those events have on those closest to them should read this book. Anyone personally involved in any way in the criminal justice system – whether as a lawyer, judge, police, prison or probation officer, journalist or offender – has a duty to do so.

Duncan Campbell

Prologue

'I've been thinking…'

WE HAD EXPECTED my father to be groggy but still able to communicate after his operation. Catherine was nine and Ruth was seven. We tried to explain that some people took longer than others to come round from an anaesthetic. The hospital staff had said there was no cause for concern and therefore we shouldn't be too worried.

Day succeeded day and he didn't recover consciousness. It was difficult to describe to our daughters the difference between being asleep and being unconscious.

Ruth came home from school one day and said: 'I've been thinking about Grandad. However hard anybody tries, they can't understand what somebody else is feeling or know what they are thinking.'

Chapter One
The news

THE DOORBELL RANG. We glanced at each other to see who had eaten the most. I went to the front door, leaving my husband to complete his evening meal.

It is only a few steps from our dining room along the diamond-patterned hall carpet to the front door of our 1930s end-of-terrace house. Ahead I saw the outline of a man, framed in the glass panel of the door. I switched on the porch light and opened the door.

There were two other people standing behind the man I had seen; they were outside the pool of light. The man in front of me had on a dark coat over a suit. He held out a small wallet to show me his card. It was 6.30 p.m. on Friday, 2 February 1990.

'Police, Enfield. Can we come in, please?' I stood aside to let him and the other two officers in. 'Is your husband at home?' he asked. I called Vic to join us. 'Is it about Ruth?' I asked. She was the only member of our family who lived in Enfield.

'Can we go into your front room?' he said, and introduced himself as Inspector van Thal of the Metropolitan Police.

The five of us moved into our front room, jostling slightly in the confined space. I thought that Ruth must have been involved in a car accident.

Vic and I stood side by side in the middle of our front room. We invited the police officers to sit down. Two of them sat on the settee. Inspector van Thal was still standing. We looked at him, hearts thudding, awaiting his news.

'I am very sorry. I have come to tell you that your daughter,

Ruth, is dead. She has been found in suspicious circumstances.'

Vic and I moved into each other's arms. We clung, swaying slightly, and it seemed as if many minutes went by before we dared to let go of each other. My mind couldn't absorb the fact that our youngest daughter was dead.

My first words when we separated were: 'Would anyone like a cup of tea?' I stumbled into the kitchen, my hands automatically performing the routine tasks of filling the kettle, setting out five mugs. Everything seemed strangely still. I couldn't hear any conversation from the front room. When I returned to distribute the tea, I asked if we could go and see Ruth.

Inspector van Thal shook his head very quickly. 'No, that isn't possible.'

'Where is she? I want to see her.'

'She is at the police mortuary.'

'What else can you tell us?'

'Nothing more at present; someone will contact you tomorrow with more information. Would you like us to telephone your GP or someone from the local Victim Support group?'

I wanted them to go; I wanted to be with Vic; I wanted Ruth to be alive.

The inspector asked, 'Is there anything we can do to help?' We couldn't think of anything. He advised us to make sure that we were at home the next morning.

By now Vic was sitting in his chair looking stunned. I showed the police officers out. They had been in our house for less than half an hour.

'We must go and tell Catherine,' Vic said. Our elder daughter had married in 1988 and moved to a town to the north of us. We both felt it was right to go quickly and tell Catherine face to face rather than telephone her.

'Will you be all right to drive?' I asked. Vic nodded and we put our coats on. The dishes from our evening meal were still on the table.

In the car my thoughts were full of Ruth. We had been expecting to see her over the weekend, as her twenty-fourth birthday would be on 6 February, in four days' time. I tried not to distract Vic. Our only conversation during the half-hour journey was to discuss who would tell Catherine; we agreed that he would. If there was time, we would also go to see my mother, and I would tell her.

*

How could Ruth be dead? She had always been such a lively presence in our family.

A mischievous child who appeared as the Virgin Mary in the infant-school nativity play holding 'Baby Jesus', with the doll's naked bottom sticking out of the folded sheet. A rebellious adolescent whose left ear was pierced so many times that we used to tease her by saying it would finish up with pinked edges. She had left home when she was twenty-two to share a rented house with a friend she had known since her schooldays. She'd established herself as a training officer helping women who had been unemployed to regain confidence and new skills before returning to work.

Only a few days before she had been at our home saying she was thinking about the possibility of moving back in with us so that she could sort out some problems. Why hadn't we said immediately, 'We'll come and help you pack'? Maybe if we had, she would still be alive. We hadn't wanted to undermine her independence and, if we were being honest, we enjoyed having the house to ourselves, re-establishing ourselves as a couple whose parental responsibilities had been largely fulfilled. I had even felt rather smug at the way in which both our daughters had left home of their own choice, in their own time.

*

The roads were quiet; the Friday evening rush hour was over. It was a cold, wintry, windy evening.

I thought about Catherine and the blow that was about to hit her. She and Ruth were very different, physically and temperamentally, and since Catherine's marriage and Ruth's move to Enfield they hadn't seen a great deal of each other. They had both been busy establishing their working lives and their new homes.

Catherine's husband, Stephen, came to the door and we followed him into the kitchen where they had been eating their evening meal. Vic didn't hesitate. He went straight to Catherine, put his arms around her and said, 'We've come to tell you that Ruth is dead.' She cried immediately and Stephen rushed to her. The four of us hugged and patted each other; we couldn't find any words of comfort.

We couldn't tell them much because we knew so little ourselves. 'How did she die?' asked Catherine. We didn't know but we assumed that someone had killed her. 'Did she die quickly?' We didn't know. 'Where did she die?' We didn't know.

We said that we were going to see my mother on our way home, and Catherine and Stephen decided to come with us, but to travel in their own car. This was another half-hour journey, nearly back to our own home. Back in our car, Vic and I asked each other anxiously about Catherine's reaction and how we thought she and my mother would cope.

My father had died in 1980 and my mother had lived by

herself ever since. She had had a hard life. Her father died when she was six; my father was disabled, and my brother has severe learning difficulties. She had always been very dependent on me, and at times I resented this and wished she had a circle of friends and independent social activities. She was fearful about many things, some of them quite irrational, and she regularly sought reassurance from me. Ruth had always been far more able than I was to jolly my mother out of her anxieties; she could be quite direct in saying how foolish some of the fears were without being unkind. I had sometimes asked Ruth to mediate on my behalf when the pressures from my mother became too great. She also helped my mother in practical ways. She had redecorated the bathroom in my mother's maisonette and often took her to garden centres. On these journeys my mother clung precariously to the door strap in Ruth's battered, blue Fiat, in which the passenger seat was inclined to move of its own accord.

I rang my mother's doorbell. She answered, looking delighted to see the four of us for an unexpected visit. But when I told her about Ruth, her happiness turned to anguish. She gasped and curled into a small ball in her chair, crying, 'It should have been me! It should have been me!'

I held her and rocked her and let her cry until she gradually quietened.

'Do you want to come home with us and stay overnight?' I asked. She said, 'No, I would rather be in my own bed.' We lived within a few minutes' drive, on the other side of the town. We left saying that she should telephone us if she needed us and we would call her in the morning. Catherine and Stephen returned to their home.

*

While we had been away from our home, the wind had gathered force and changed direction. It howled in the chimneys as I moved between the front room and the kitchen, mechanically picking up the mugs and then clearing the table in the dining room.

'We must get some rest and go to bed,' Vic said. We got ready for bed and he fell asleep quite quickly. I envied his being able to lose consciousness.

Lying in bed, I went over and over what Inspector van Thal had said and suddenly thought that maybe what he had really meant was that Ruth had committed suicide. If she had in fact taken her own life, how could we not have realised that she was so unhappy? She did have problems, but they were on their way to being resolved, and she had talked to us quite openly about them. A relationship had broken up just a month before, and she was waiting for her former partner, Tom, to move out of the house. As ever, she had financial problems, but they weren't insurmountable.

How could I not have known at some subconscious level that she had died? Why had I been away mid-week, returning to find her cheery message on the answerphone saying she would drop in to see if I was at home? That was the last time I had heard her voice, and the message had already been erased. I found it difficult to breathe, felt a great pain in my chest. Sobs rose from deep within and tears flowed, soaking my pillow. Vic was still soundly asleep and I briefly considered waking him, to ask to be held in his arms and comforted and to comfort him. But no, it was better that he slept while he could.

The questions we hadn't asked the police went round and round in my head. How did she die? How long did it take? Where was she when she died? Was she alone? When did it happen? And most of all, *why* did it happen? I couldn't sleep.

And then I thought: was it really her? Had they made a mistake? How could someone with so much life and so much to do with it be dead? The questions circled round and round, keeping time with the frantic wind crying, 'No, no, no.'

Eventually, I did sleep, but woke very early. It was still completely dark outside.

I went downstairs and got out one of our family photograph albums. It covered the time when Ruth was at junior school. I looked at her running fast at a school sports day; standing proudly in her Red Cross uniform; at a safari park where we had gone to celebrate Catherine's birthday. Lots of happy memories. In every photograph her energy and commitment to what she was doing was apparent, even when she was making a determined attempt not to be photographed.

When Vic got up, I was still sitting with the album.

'Shall we have some breakfast?' he said. I looked at him in disbelief. How could we eat when Ruth was dead? He was gently insistent that we needed to eat, to nourish ourselves to face the visit from the police later in the day and whatever else lay ahead of us.

I found it hard to swallow, pushing small pieces of toast into my mouth and softening them with sips of tea, looking at the chair where Ruth used to sit opposite me when she still lived with us.

I phoned my mother after giving up the struggle to eat breakfast, and she said she was all right. She had asked a neighbour to be with her until we phoned with the news from the police. Catherine and Stephen arrived. Her face was white and puffy; Stephen's arm was curled protectively around her waist.

Just after 10 a.m., the doorbell rang, and Vic let in a burly middle-aged man, dressed in a mackintosh, accompanied by a slim young woman. Detective Inspector Geoff Parratt said how sorry he was that Ruth had died and explained that he was the senior officer in charge of the case.

He said, 'We have a man in custody helping us with our enquiries and we expect to make a charge later in the day.' We asked if the man in custody was Ruth's former partner, Tom, and were relieved to hear that it wasn't. He couldn't tell us the name of the man who was in custody in case he was released without being charged with an offence. He said that Ruth had died quickly and would not have suffered.

It was a brief visit. He left after checking that we would be at home all day, and promised to phone us as soon as he had further news.

Catherine and Stephen wanted to stay with us until the news came through from the police, so we had some lunch together. Not long after we had finished eating, Geoff Parratt telephoned. 'We have charged Andrew Steel with murdering Ruth.' This was the first time that the word murder had been used, and it was the first time I heard the name Andrew Steel.

'Who is he? Did Ruth know him?' I asked.

'We think she did,' Geoff replied.

'How did he kill her?'

'He stabbed her.'

'Where did she die?'

'In her home, in Enfield.'

'When did it happen?'

'We think it was very early yesterday morning. We'll contact you when we have more information.'

I relayed the responses to the questions to Vic, Catherine and Stephen. None of us had ever heard the name Andrew Steel.

I wondered what was happening to Andrew Steel's family. Their situation would be as painful as ours but in a different way. But their son was alive and our daughter was dead. I also wondered how Andrew Steel was feeling. If he had killed Ruth, was he remorseful, was he ashamed, and was he afraid of what would happen to him?

*

Later that day we decided to go to see Vic's family. Most of them live in Kent. We went first to see Vic's sister Pat and her family. We had often said that Ruth was very like Pat, generous to a fault, the kind of person that others in trouble would turn to for support and advice. Pat and Ruth were very close, and it was very painful to break the news to her. One of our nieces cried so much and so hysterically that we thought we might have to call a doctor.

We discussed how we should break the news to Vic's mother, whose health was frail. It was already dark when we followed Pat and Ron in their car to see Vic's other sister, Christine, and her family. There more tears fell, and the shock of the news made it hard to convince them that Ruth really was dead. By then, it was too late to go to see Vic's mother, and we decided to phone her doctor for advice and return to see her the next day.

Vic's mother took the news stoically. Her life, like my mother's, had been punctuated by untimely bereavements. Vic's sister, Christine, came with us and stayed on to be with Vic's mother after we left.

*

When we got home, the answerphone tape was full. We recorded a new message. It started conventionally enough:

'This is the answerphone of Vic and Lesley Moreland. We are sorry that we are not able to take your call at the moment. Please leave a message, giving your name and telephone number, and we will get back to you as soon as possible.' It continued: 'If you are calling about our daughter, Ruth, we hope you will understand that the only way we can cope with calls for the time being is to leave the answerphone on. We would very much appreciate any message you may care to leave for us. We are listening to the messages regularly. Please speak slowly and clearly after the tone.'

The phone rang many times, and I made many phone calls myself. Over and over again I said: 'I'm phoning with some bad news. It's about Ruth. She is dead. A man has been charged with murdering her.' After phoning members of our large extended family and our closest friends, I was exhausted. The reactions were a mixture of disbelief, horror, grief and anger. Those I had phoned broke the news in turn to others.

I imagined a huge sound wave expanding further and further into infinity as more and more people heard the news.

On Sunday afternoon, Catherine and Stephen arrived to let us know that Stephen had been asked by the police to identify Ruth formally, and they had been to the mortuary that morning. Catherine had been advised not to see Ruth but to remember her as she was when she was alive. Apparently, Geoff Parratt had taken Stephen to one side on the previous day to ask if he would be willing to do this. The police thought it would be too hard for either Vic or me to identify her. Catherine, too, had harboured hopes that there had been a mistake, that when Stephen came back he would say it wasn't Ruth he had seen. But he nodded sadly, and said she had a black eye and a bruise over her cheek but otherwise looked quite peaceful.

I was confused at this news. I had asked to see Ruth and had been told that I could not. Stephen had been placed in a difficult situation. I felt that he and Catherine had been forced to be deceitful, as they had been advised not to tell us about the visit to the mortuary until afterwards.

*

On Monday, Vic and I contacted the people we worked with to explain what had happened. Vic's employers suggested that he should contact them when he felt able to return to work. The senior partner in the management consultancy where I worked immediately offered to inform my colleagues and clients. I asked him to transfer my clients to other consultants.

The phone rang more and more, and cards, letters and flowers started to arrive. A most persistent caller was a man from an animal sanctuary. Ruth had three cats: Lucy, Ben and Barbie. Ben and Barbie were brother and sister and had come from the sanctuary. He wanted to know if the cats were being looked after and if Barbie had been spayed. How he traced us I don't know. The cats were being well looked after by neighbours. I didn't know if Barbie had been spayed. I asked him not to call again.

Most of the letter-writers had difficulty finding words to express their feelings. 'I feel absolutely devastated by the news of Ruth. I cannot begin to imagine how you are feeling and really don't know what to say to you.' This was a theme repeated in many ways. The letters that shared people's memories of Ruth were particularly precious.

We found a home-baked fruit cake on the doorstep with a note offering help. Another friend brought a bottle of brandy. Vic is teetotal and I am only a very occasional drinker, even more rarely of spirits, but she felt we needed something to help with the shock. One of Ruth's primary-school teachers sent a tape of John Rutter's *Requiem*. The note with the tape said, 'It reminds me of Ruth because it is a mixture of styles, modern and classical, taking the best of both, and she was the same, always her own person setting her own standards even as a seven year old.'

I had to go shopping for groceries. I was in a daze as I went around Sainsbury's. One aisle had shelves full of Easter eggs. Ruth had complained because we didn't continue to buy Easter eggs for her and Catherine once they had started at secondary school. I had begrudged wasting money on the packaging, and preferred to give her and Catherine money for a treat of their choice. Now I wished and wished I hadn't deprived her of this small gift. I walked quickly around the store, just buying the items on my list. I had to queue for several minutes before unloading the trolley. The assistant passed the items to me as she checked them. As I started to pack the groceries I heard a sharp crack. A jar of tomato paste had shattered. Red oozed down the moving rubber belt, forming a rolling pool before disappearing under the metal bar. The fragments of glass gathered together, sharp surfaces glistening in the viscous sauce. I couldn't speak and didn't reach out to help move the shards of glass or mop up the smeared contents of the jar. It took all my self-control to wait while the packaging was wiped with a damp cloth, the shopping was packed and the bill paid. I shook all the way home.

*

Later that day, Vic and I discussed the many things that had to be done. The agent for the rented house in Enfield would have to be contacted, and all the utilities advised. Ruth's possessions would have to be removed from the house and decisions made about what to do with them. We knew from our long shared past that we were likely to have different ideas at times about how we wanted to do things.

Ours is a marriage of contrasting temperaments. Vic is a quiet, reflective person and tends to express his feelings more through his actions than his words. I am more outgoing and seek information about new experiences from as many sources as I can find. We agreed that we would need to let each other achieve what we wanted to do in the way we wanted to do it. It wouldn't be possible for us to do everything together anyway.

Vic went to see a local funeral director, only to learn that we would not be able to make any funeral arrangements until the police advised us that Ruth's body could be released. In their experience, this could mean waiting for weeks or even months. 'But she's our daughter,' I said. 'Why can't we hold the funeral now?' It felt as if we were being pushed aside, as if Ruth was no longer part of our family. Not only was she dead, we had no choice as to when we could hold her funeral.

Later in the week, Catherine and I went to Ruth's rented house to bring home some of her possessions. It was in a road of 1930s housing, very similar to our own home. It had the same layout: in through the front door, the kitchen ahead, living room and dining room to the left. The wall between the living and dining rooms had been removed to produce one long, thin room.

It was hard to walk through the front door into the empty house. On the mat there were a few envelopes, some obviously cards for Ruth for the birthday she didn't live to celebrate. No cats came to greet us. The house was unusually tidy. We learned afterwards that two of her friends had been in to tidy up after the police had completed their work. On the dining-room table there was a tray full of painted models that Ruth and a friend had been making to sell at a car-boot sale.

We didn't know which room Ruth had died in. Was it in the kitchen, the front room, upstairs? We looked into each room and saw no signs of violence, no broken furniture or stains. In the bathroom we noticed that a section of the vinyl flooring had been removed.

We went into Ruth's bedroom. Her Auntie Pat had asked for the silver bracelet she had given Ruth some years before. Catherine found it and also the earrings that she and Stephen had given to Ruth to wear at their wedding in 1988. They were with other things that were precious to Ruth, carefully placed together on a shelf in her wardrobe. The gold chain Catherine had given her for her twenty-first birthday wasn't there. We assumed that she had been wearing it when she died. It was horrible to go through her personal possessions; we felt as if we were invading her privacy, and yet I also wanted to find things that would keep her presence near. I found and packed her Filofax, her make-up bag and the notes she had been making for new course material for work.

I also brought home the photographs on display in the house, mainly of family members, many taken on our silver wedding anniversary in 1987. She had bought frames for the photos and placed them on her bedside table and on the mantlepiece in the front room.

Tom, Ruth's ex-partner, arrived to pick up his clothes and records. He was obviously ill at ease. He told us that he had been arrested on Friday and held at the police station overnight. He said, 'Andrew Steel was a friend of mine; I brought him to the house, and that is how Ruth met him. I have no idea why Andy killed Ruth. Ruth had always been helpful to him. The three of us shared evenings with other friends here, watching videos, having meals together.'

I moved towards him, gave him a hug and said how hard it was for all us. His body stiffened and he didn't respond. He didn't want to talk any more. He gathered his belongings, saying that he was going to stay with friends rather than returning to his parents' home.

Chapter Two
A long day

DESPITE EVERYTHING I had been told by the police and by my son-in-law Stephen, a small part of me still hung on to the extremely remote possibility that it had all been a horrible mistake. Ruth had played tricks on us before – would she suddenly appear, giggling, and say, 'Got you going there, didn't I?' She would never have done anything so cruel, but I still had this irrational, microscopic shred of hope that the body at the mortuary would not be hers.

I telephoned to ask the police again if I could see Ruth. I wasn't the only one who wanted to see her. Vic's sister Pat, Ruth's work colleague Sheila, and James, a young man Ruth had met a few weeks before she died, had also asked if they could go to the mortuary. Neither Vic nor Catherine wanted to go, but Vic wanted me to ask if we could have a lock of Ruth's hair.

The police had advised me several times that it would be best for me to remember Ruth as she was when she was alive, and urged me not to see her. It felt as if they were trying to fob me off in order to protect themselves. I persisted, explaining that the only way for me to be convinced that she really was dead would be to see her. I also wanted to hold her and to say goodbye. Reluctantly, they agreed, and arrangements were made for the four of us to go the mortuary in Hornsey on 8 February – almost a week after Ruth's murder.

Pat came to our house in the early afternoon with her husband, Ron. I put a chicken casserole in the oven on the automatic timer so that we would have a hot meal ready when we returned. Matt Miller, a young-looking, dark-haired detective sergeant, arrived and took us to Hornsey in an unmarked police car. It was a clear, bright day, and as Matt drove through the North London suburbs, I saw the turning to Alexandra Palace and asked if we could take that route, as Pat had never seen the view over London from that high point. From the car we could see right across the city, the ground falling away from us steeply into a rounded pit containing millions of people whose daily lives were continuing in their familiar patterns. I was filled with dread, fearing that it would be Ruth, hoping that it wouldn't be Ruth I would see at the end of this journey.

The mortuary building at Hornsey was utilitarian, with no soft surfaces anywhere in its interior. Pat, Sheila and I were told in the waiting room that we would be taken one at a time to see Ruth. James was being brought to the mortuary by another police officer. I was the first to go to see Ruth and I walked up the stairs almost eagerly. Entering the room, I stood between Matt and the coroner's officer, supported by their arms, our bodies touching, to wait for the curtain in front of us to be pulled aside. Matt explained that Ruth would be lying on a plinth behind a glass screen facing towards us. 'Are you ready?' he said. I was ready – but first I had to ask them to put me down. They were holding me so tightly that my feet had left the floor. I suppose that both men must have been worried that I might fall, and were anxious to keep me upright.

The curtain was drawn back. The glass was immediately in front of me, blocking off any access to the area behind it. There was no doubt that it was Ruth lying on the plinth, several feet behind the glass. I could only see her face, slightly tilted towards us, a choirboy-like ruff of white fabric around her neck. There were bruises on her face, a swelling around her left eye and her beautiful hair was untidy.

I knew the first post-mortem had been done; I knew she would be cold; I knew it was likely that behind the screen the smell of chemicals would pervade the air. But I still wanted to hold my daughter. I touched the glass and traced her face, trying desperately to imprint her image in my memory. I felt frozen, wanting to ask if it was possible to go behind the screen, looking from side to side to see where the access might be. I will always regret not asking. I said nothing, inhibited by the presence of the two police officers. Unspoken thoughts rolled around inside my head. Our two bodies had been joined until her birth and now at her death I was being denied the opportunity to touch her, to hold her and say goodbye. I stood, silent, for several minutes and then indicated that I was ready to leave.

★

I asked about the lock of Ruth's hair. A large man, whose body filled the doorframe, dressed in plain clothes, appeared with a small package in his hands. With great tenderness, he gave it to me, and I was very touched to see when I looked inside that the lock of hair was carefully held together with a piece of ribbon. I buried my nose in it and breathed in the faint scent of her hair conditioner.

Before we left the mortuary, I was briefly introduced to James, Ruth's recently met friend, who was white-faced and trembling with strain. This was the first time we had met, but I already had good feelings towards him as Ruth had said, 'He treats me with respect', something she had not experienced much in her previous relationships with men. He worked for the same company and they had discussed their ambitions for the future in employment training.

Matt took Pat, Sheila and me in his car. First he would drop Sheila at her home so that she would be there when her daughters returned from school. I knew that Ruth had enjoyed working with Sheila and that they had developed a friendship outside work. We didn't talk about the visit to the mortuary during the drive. We tried to make conversation, but it wasn't easy. Pat and I had known each other for many years; Sheila hadn't met any of us, and Matt was driving. He came to the rescue. We learned that he was studying for examinations that he hoped would lead to him being promoted to the rank of inspector, and that he had a new baby son. Images of Ruth at the mortuary suffused everything for me – what had been concealed beneath that white cloth, why was her head at such a strange angle? The ending of uncertainty: Ruth was dead.

Then Matt took Pat and me to the home of Ruth's employer, Moira, where James would be brought by another police officer. Moira wanted to discuss a celebration of Ruth's life to be organised by the company.

*

I had never met Moira, the managing director of the company that Ruth worked for. I had only spoken to her on the telephone, since Ruth had died. She had been to the house before us and had taken Ruth's clothes from the laundry basket and washed and ironed them. When they were returned to us, I was very uncomfortable about this well-intended action. I felt it had deprived me of contact with the last clothes she wore. I didn't want to hurt Moira's feelings by saying this, but wasn't comfortable at the prospect of meeting her.

She gave us tea and biscuits in her large front room. Well-upholstered settees faced a coffee table near the front window, and a big dining table stood at the other end of the room. Her teenage daughters peered curiously around the door from the hall.

We were there for a long time before James arrived. I was getting anxious about the time we had been away from home, and found it difficult to talk to Moira, who was describing the impact of Ruth's death on her and her colleagues. The company was small and recently formed, so relationships were close. She said that the staff and the trainees were distraught. The news had spread rapidly and many of the women who had attended Ruth's earlier courses were coming to the offices to ask if she really was dead, and then needing to be comforted.

When James arrived, with a female police officer called Tracy, he and I sat at the large table looking at a photograph album of Catherine's wedding that I had brought with me. The photographs of Ruth showed her atypically dressed in a bridesmaid's gown of blue satin, her hair piled up in an Edwardian style. Nearby, Pat talked to Moira, and the police officers, Matt and Tracy, were talking to each other.

I asked James if he could tell me what he knew about what had happened on the Friday that Ruth died. He said, 'Ruth hadn't arrived for work. Sheila was worried and telephoned several times and got no reply. When I arrived at the office from the other branch of the company later in the morning, Sheila was frantic. We told Moira that we would go to the house. We thought that perhaps Ruth was ill; too ill to get the phone. Sheila knew she was on her own, as Ruth had told her that the tenant was away on holiday and Tom was staying with another friend overnight.' Ruth had been with Sheila at her home during the Thursday evening working on some new course material. Sheila had suggested that Ruth should stay with her overnight, but Ruth declined, saying that she had to go home to feed the cats.

'The curtains were still drawn when we got to the house.' James continued. 'We knocked at the front door and rattled the windows. There was no response, so we decided to go and have a sandwich and discuss what to do next. When we returned, the front door was wide open and there were two young men in the front garden: one was Tom. The other man was shouting and screaming.

'Tom told me that Ruth was dead and in her bedroom. I ran upstairs, telling Sheila to stay downstairs. There was a lot of blood. When I came down, I asked Tom if the police had been called. He said he had phoned them but I phoned again as there was no sign of anyone arriving.' He added, 'She wasn't sexually attacked,' as if that would be a consolation.

James asked if we could meet again, just the two of us, and I agreed it would be helpful.

*

We rejoined the others, and Moira started to talk about the plans the company were making for a ceremony to celebrate Ruth's life.

'We've decided to hire a theatre to accommodate all the people who want to come. We'll make a collection and send the money to the charities that Ruth supported.'

'But we still don't know when we'll be able to arrange the funeral,' I said. 'I can't tell you if I could come.' I didn't even know if I could face such an occasion; it felt wrong to be considering a celebration organised by other people before her family had been able to hold her funeral.

It was now early evening. I was feeling exhausted and wanted to be on my own, to think about what I had seen at the mortuary, to secure my final encounter with Ruth in my memory. Moira was talking about the possibility of naming the company's new building after Ruth. The thought of a building being named after her seemed ridiculous – very far from how I imagined Ruth would want to be remembered.

Matt drove Pat and me back to my house. The smell as we opened the door told me that the casserole hadn't burned, despite our late return.

Vic and I divided the lock of hair so that we each had some, and I divided mine further to give some to James when we met.

Chapter Three
Visits, a statement and a letter

THE DAY AFTER my visit to the mortuary, Vic and I went to see the letting agent for the house and the manager at Ruth's bank to see what needed to be done about her financial affairs. We telephoned in advance to advise them that Ruth had died.

The letting agent gave the briefest of acknowledgements that we had suffered a terrible bereavement. We were told that the house should be emptied of personal possessions and the furniture replaced in the original positions within a week. I said, 'We can't do it. We don't remember where the furniture was when Ruth and her friend moved in eighteen months ago.' We also didn't know the whereabouts of one of the lodgers, who had been away on holiday when Ruth died.

At the bank, the manager was out of his depth in dealing with us. He asked many questions about the circumstances of Ruth's death, wanting to know about her injuries. We had very little information ourselves and certainly had no wish to discuss details with a stranger. We felt his approach was intrusive and insensitive. He said he needed some formal proof before he could arrange to stop payments from her accounts; we had nothing in writing.

The weekend before Ruth died, we had been to hang the curtains in our 20-foot narrow boat, which Vic had fitted out himself. This was the completion of two years of weekend and holiday work. Pat and Ron had come with us and we had had a very happy day, rounded off by a meal in a restaurant. We had enjoyed being four adults together after many years of shared family occasions with our children. After leaving the bank, we went home and packed quickly to go to the boat to get away, to be by ourselves. I didn't really want to see the boat – it contained the clock and kitchen equipment that Ruth had given Vic for Christmas – but I made myself get on board and we stayed there for the night.

On Sunday morning, 10 February, I met James for the second time at a friend's house. We talked about Ruth. His memories were packed into a brief but intense encounter of only a few weeks; mine were spread over nearly twenty-four years. Although he was very distressed, I could see that he had maturity far beyond that of Ruth's previous partners. He spoke of having 'found the other half of my sixpence'. Although they had known each other for only a few weeks, he felt that he had met someone he wanted to be with for the rest of his life. From what Ruth had said about him, I knew that she was more tentative, anxious not to commit herself too soon after the break-up of the relationship with Tom. James was bitterly angry about her death: 'She's up there somewhere, bloody furious at what has happened.' We agreed to keep in touch and to support each other, and I gave him copies of some recent photographs of Ruth and part of the lock of her hair.

*

Letters, phone calls and flowers continued to come daily. Florists generally associate delivering flowers to private homes with happy occasions. 'Someone's birthday?' one deliveryman said brightly. My response was to burst into tears, snatch the flowers and close the door.

A comment that caught me completely off guard was, 'Well, never mind.' Never mind? When every part of me minded in a manner never before experienced.

I had to learn quickly to be aware of the intention of what

people said, even if their words were clumsy, and to appreciate that they had made an effort to say something.

Some comments were less than helpful. 'Why didn't you make sure that Ruth was not alone in the house?' I can imagine Ruth's reaction if we had asked her to let us know if she would be alone. Nonetheless, the comment still stung; it implied that we had been less than caring parents.

Some people offered thoughts from their own belief systems that did not find any response in my own. Ruth was uplifted to be an 'angel', 'too good to live', or 'fulfilling her karma'. I felt her life was diminished by portraying her as someone who had risen above other people, or who was destined to die in such a cruel way.

'How are you?' or 'How do you feel?' were difficult questions to respond to. At one level the questioner seemed to be inviting the usual 'We're coping', but at another level I often sensed that they were not really inviting a full response and wanted to protect themselves from knowing about the depths of my grief. As my feelings were volatile, I found it more helpful if people added a time boundary to their enquiry — 'How are you today?'

Many people wanted to help, to show their support in a practical way, and yet were hesitant to intrude. Phrases such as 'Let me know if there is anything I can do', or, 'Do call me', were too vague to be helpful. A few people got quite agitated if their offer of non-specific help was not taken up and almost insisted that we found something for them to do — a demand on our limited energies that was not welcome.

It was difficult to think of things that people could do to help, and I had done things myself before considering whether someone else might have been only too happy to do them for me. My library books were overdue. When I took them back to the library, the librarian commented that it was very unusual for me to be late returning them. 'Have you had some problems?' she enquired kindly. 'Yes, my daughter has been murdered,' I blurted out, not prefacing this bald statement with any gentler phrase. My communication skills were diminished, too. It helped me to understand why other people made inappropriate comments.

Other people wanted to come to see us to share their feelings about Ruth's death. One was a young man who had been at college with Ruth and was working as a police photographer. We were horrified to learn that in his professional capacity he had been called to Ruth's house. As soon as he went in he recognised the photographs on the mantlepiece; he had taken them himself on our silver wedding anniversary. When he realised that it was Ruth he was to photograph, he asked if another police photographer could be used. He was told that no other photographer was available, so he had to go through with it. He had also taken the photographs at Catherine's wedding, so he knew our family well.

He had brought the negatives of the anniversary and wedding photographs with him, as he wanted us to have them.

*

The police asked me to give a 'witness statement', and Vic and I went to the police station and met Matt Miller there. Before making the statement, we went to see Ruth's car, which had been taken by the police for their investigations. Inside, the car was still decorated with Christmas tinsel. Work papers, magazines and tapes were on the back seat and floor. I had bought her the used, French-mustard-coloured car the previous summer when her beloved blue Fiat, a gift from a friend, was finally deemed beyond repair. We were trying to work out the logistics of disposing of Ruth's car. We only had one car ourselves, and it had been many years since I had driven. Matt offered to do it for us. This kindness was such a relief, appreciated even more as we realised he would be doing it in his own time, not as part of his official role as a police officer.

As we walked through the police station we were taken to the incident room and saw white boards nearly covering one wall. Ruth's name was at the top, written in capital letters with a broad felt-tip pen. Notes and maps covered the boards in a variety of colours.

The three of us went to a small, stark room, and Matt gently explained that they needed a brief background account of Ruth's life. He asked questions, wrote down a summary of my responses and read the statement back to me.

He asked where Ruth was born, where she went to school and about her social and working life. In his own words, the final sentence of the statement said, 'She was, in every sense of the word, a lovely girl.'

He told us that Andrew Steel had been remanded in custody and would remain in prison until the trial – he hadn't been granted bail. We also learned that the coroner's inquest had been held on the same day that we had been to see the letting agent and the bank manager. I was very upset that we hadn't been told about this, as we might have found out more about Ruth's injuries if we had attended the inquest, and other information might well have been revealed. Matt said this would have been unlikely and the hearing would have been very brief.

★

A few days later I was on my own in the house when the post arrived. On the mat were several letters, one of them with an Enfield postmark.

Inside the tightly packed small envelope were several pages of lined notepaper. The letter was from Ruth's neighbour.

Ruth's passing has shocked the close.

I've wanted to get in touch with you, but the police declined to give me your address. They told me though that they would tell me when the funeral would be, so I could collect for flowers, as I told them Ruth always gave generously to others in the close.

First of all I must say, I'm still in a state of shock, after the sudden death of my husband 3 months ago, from a severe heart attack in the night, a fit man, never a day's illness in his life.

Ruth offered to cut the grass for me, and sent me a lovely card with all her love.

I haven't slept much since Charlie died, so I was soon awakened to Ruth's, what I now know, to have been Ruth's last screams. Then silence. Then a lot of noise, which I thought were perhaps the lodgers fighting or perhaps some burst pipes, as there was a lot of running up and down the stairs, which I know you have to be quick to turn mains water off. Then after a while a man's voice called out, and the front door went with an almighty Bang. I got up to look out of the front window but didn't see anyone.

I thought no more of it. Next day I went to my daughter's to mind my grandson for the day, he has been a great comfort to me after Charlie's death, Charlie adored him.

When I came back that evening, I saw a lot of police about, and before I went to bed, I thought I had better see what was going on, so I phoned my other neighbour. She came in to me, like a ghost, and told me they had 'found' Ruth. That's all I know, no details, and I've told everyone not to tell me any, I couldn't bear it.

I have got to live with the rest of my life knowing I heard her last screams. If it is any comfort to you at all, I am also sharing your intense grief which must be immense for you.

This second shock, on top of Charlie's, is taking its toll on me.

I have had many visits from the C.I.D. and I may be needed to give evidence, as at that time between 4—6 in the morning, it seems I was the only one, who heard anything. Although they haven't told me much, or what the motive was, or anything.

They are worried about me being alone, and have sent someone from Victim Support to see me.

From what I have heard since, it appears, I have seen the man, who did it, who sometimes visited the house.

I did warn Ruth once, to choose her friends and lodgers carefully. My husband and I thought she was very vulnerable in there.

She seemed a nice girl herself, loved her cats and soft toys, it's a tragic loss of a young life, who apparently was interested in others' welfare.

My heart goes out to you her parents and her sister, words can't express my feelings, God Rest her soul. I'm only glad they got the man.

May God give you strength to see you through the coming days as I'm sure he did me recently.

I reread the letter several times. What jumped out at me was the proof that Ruth *had* suffered — she had screamed. The assurances we had been given that she had not suffered were not true. I hadn't thought they could be true, but here was graphic evidence of her terror and pain.

Someone had heard her and had done nothing. Someone full of her own grief, mainly concerned in protecting herself, offered her suffering as a comfort to us.

I remembered Ruth talking about her neighbours, who had lived in their house for all their married life. They sounded like very conventional people who resented any intrusion into the quiet pattern of their lives. Why had her neighbour assumed that the noise she heard was 'the lodgers fighting'?

Why did she presume to make judgements about Ruth being 'vulnerable' in her own home? These comments made her condolences ring hollow.

I will never know, and neither will she, whether, if she had telephoned the emergency services when she heard the screams, Ruth's life could have been saved.

'Oh, my poor baby, oh, my poor baby,' I kept thinking, never having referred to Ruth as a baby since she was out of nappies. A night owl rather than a lark, she would have been asleep when Andrew Steel entered the house. Between four and six in the morning is a low time for most people. How frightened she must have been; but she couldn't have realised that her life was at risk.

The day after the arrival of the neighbour's letter, Vic and I went again to Ruth's house in Enfield. Pat and Ron came with us. Two of their daughters were setting up their own homes, and they took Ruth's furniture. We packed her remaining possessions into our car.

Various family members and friends had asked for mementos. In asking for tangible objects, I sensed that many people wanted to hold on to part of Ruth and their memories of her impact on their lives. While no one made unreasonable demands, it was difficult to go through her personal things and consider what would be appropriate for each person.

We put aside Ruth's teddy bear and her food processor for my mother, and her television for Vic's mother. We searched the whole house but still couldn't find the gold chain necklace.

Vic and I went to Catherine and Stephen's the next evening, taking most of Ruth's possessions with us. We decided that her outer clothing should go to a charity shop, and Stephen offered to take it to a shop in the town where he worked so that we would not have to run the risk of coming across any of it in our town. As we sorted through her clothes and records, the two kittens played nearby. I looked at them and thought that if Ruth hadn't taken them in, she might still be alive; she had only returned home that night because they needed to be fed.

Chapter Four

From a celebration to a funeral

NEARLY TWO WEEKS after Ruth's death, the police could still give us no indication of when we would be able to hold her funeral. We had been thinking about what form the service should take. I had worked for a bereavement charity, the Stillbirth and Neonatal Death Society (SANDS), and through that work I knew a hospital chaplain. I decided to go and ask him for advice. As far as we knew, Ruth had no particular religious beliefs. The people attending the funeral would be representing many different aspects of Ruth's life and ours; and were from a wide range of faiths or none at all.

Vic returned to work on 14 February, the day I went to see the chaplain. During the eleven days since we had heard the news of Ruth's murder, I hadn't travelled on public transport or been far from home by myself. I felt very shaky travelling among strangers. It felt as if what had happened must be apparent in my face, and I would not be able to hide it. I was worried that I would break down and cry and not be able to stop.

On the way to the hospital from the Underground station, as I was too early for the appointment, I went into a bookshop. I found a modern Book of Hours. One entry from Søren Kierkegaard's *Stages on Life's Way* struck me forcibly: 'Life can only be understood backwards; but it has to be lived forwards.' Somehow I had to focus on the meeting ahead, to ensure that Ruth's funeral would be an occasion that didn't avoid the reality of the manner of her death and yet could give comfort to the people attending.

At the hospital, I spent an hour with the chaplain, talking through the possibilities. He offered to take the service if he was available. He suggested a structure loosely based on the traditional Church of England funeral service.

Catherine and Stephen came to dinner with us that evening and we discussed and developed ideas for the service. Catherine suggested that we could read out excerpts from the letters we had received, sharing the memories that people had recalled about Ruth at various stages of her life. We wrote a letter to family, friends and colleagues, letting them know that we couldn't make arrangements for a funeral until the coroner had released her body.

*

So far, we had little idea of what had caused Ruth's death or how extensive her injuries were. The copy of the coroner's interim certificate, which arrived in a plain brown envelope, revealed very little:

> The precise medical cause of death was as follows:
> 1a Haemorrhage due to Multiple Stab and Incised Wounds.

This formal eight-word phrase gave no indication of the number or location of her wounds. It wasn't precise enough for me; it didn't provide any evidence of how long it took for Ruth to die.

I had nightmares and thought obsessively during the day about how Ruth had died. After receiving the letter from Ruth's neighbour, I was no longer able to trust the reassurances we had been given by the police. Were they trying to comfort me or protect themselves or us by saying they thought she had died quickly, or didn't they really know?

I asked a friend, who is a magistrate, to drive me to some

local woods so that we could walk and talk together. The woods have a number of paths identified by different colours. We chose one where we hoped we would encounter very few people. I talked non-stop, posing questions that she couldn't answer. 'How much had Ruth suffered?' 'How did Andrew Steel get into the house?' 'What kind of person was he?' 'What could have been going on in his life for him to attack and kill Ruth?' When I asked if it would be possible for me to see Andrew Steel in order to get some answers, she said she thought that would be very difficult, particularly before the trial had taken place.

*

It was awful to be planning a funeral for Ruth when our expectations would have been to be planning her wedding (if she were ever to do anything as conventional as to get married). My work as the director of SANDS had given me a lot of background theory about loss. During daily contact with bereaved parents, I had listened to many experiences of grief. My own life experience had not been short on bereavement and trauma, but nothing could have prepared me for the impact of what I was feeling now.

When I worked at SANDS, we had many discussions about the futility of trying to construct 'league tables' of suffering. Who was to say which kind of bereavement was the worst? Surely what matters is what a particular person feels about what has happened to them. Ruefully, I had to admit that having a beloved daughter murdered felt as if it were at the extreme end of the spectrum of bereavement. The significant difference from death due to illness or accident was that another person had taken Ruth's life.

Five years before, Ruth had been the victim of a hit-and-run car driver and was taken to hospital, unconscious, with a broken arm and leg. We didn't know where she was for two days and nights. That experience now seemed like a bizarre preparation for her death, but then we had had hope, and that hope was fulfilled. Her broken bones had mended. She had not died.

Many people asked me what I felt about Andrew Steel. My answer was that I didn't know what I felt towards him, though I knew how I felt about what he had done. I was trying hard to separate the person from the act of committing murder – a task made harder since I had no idea what kind of person he was or what his relationship had been to Ruth. As a Quaker, it also challenged my belief in 'that of God in everyone'.

Moira, Ruth's employer, phoned us to say that the company's celebration of Ruth's life would be held on 1 March. She would be sending an invitation to us and hoped we would feel able to attend. I phoned the police to ask if there was any way they could find out when Ruth's body would be released, in case we might be able to hold the funeral before the celebration. I was told that 'the defendant had exercised his right to a second post-mortem' and this was still to be conducted. I hadn't known that this was a possibility and found it hard to understand why a second post-mortem was needed.

I phoned Victim Support, an organisation which offers support to the victims of crime. I spoke to an information officer who said that prosecution and defence counsels had different objectives in preparing their briefs and could therefore ask pathologists to look for different information. The first post-mortem had been done on behalf of the Crown Prosecution Service. It was also possible that it would take time for a defence counsel to be appointed, and the defendant's right to a second post-mortem had to be respected. 'But surely there ought to be a time limit on how long families have to wait to arrange a funeral?' I said. I was told that sometimes it had taken months, and, in rare cases, years. It felt as if Ruth had been taken away from us twice, first by Andrew Steel and then by the criminal justice system.

*

Catherine and I decided we would attend the celebration organised by Ruth's employers. The company sent a car to take us to Palmers Green. 'Winter', from Vivaldi's *Four Seasons*, was playing as we entered the theatre. There was a bank of faces before us in the raised seating. We were asked to sit at the front of the auditorium, facing the audience. Some people were crying openly; others had tissues clutched tightly in their hands. The atmosphere was charged with tension.

A man with a calm, mellifluous voice gave the opening reading. He spoke of the shock, anger, confusion, hurt, guilt and, most of all, the grief felt at the news of Ruth's death. Its impact was like an earthquake in that many circles of people had been affected, her family being at the epicentre.

Readings of prose and poetry followed, each delivered by a member of staff or a trainee. It was a moving and draining occasion. Moving to see so many people who had cherished Ruth and benefited from her commitment to her work; draining to hear the eulogies for someone who was essentially quite irreverent and would probably have had some pithy comments to make if she could have been present.

*

Unknown to us, the second post-mortem took place on that day, but there was still paperwork to be completed, and it was a few days more before we heard that we could go ahead with arranging the funeral.

Vic and I went together to see our local funeral directors. They had arranged my father's funeral some years before. The chaplain who had offered to take the service was going to the United States and wouldn't be back for some weeks, so I asked their advice about a suitable person to hold the funeral. They suggested a local woman priest who they said would be flexible and sensitive in conducting the kind of service we wanted.

Just then, a postal strike was declared and the logistics of informing everyone about the funeral became very complicated. We had to make more phone calls and ask for people's help in informing others. I walked for miles locally to deliver the notices about the arrangements.

RUTH'S FUNERAL WILL BE HELD AT:
West Herts Crematorium, High Elms Lane, Watford
on Tuesday, 13th March 1990 at 2.30 p.m.
   If you would like to join us, you will be very welcome.
We realise that some people who would like to come may not
be able to do so. We would like to thank Ruth's friends and
colleagues who have sent donations in her memory to the
Brittle Bones Society and/or SENSE – the National Deaf-Blind
and Rubella Association.
   We would ask that flowers are sent from family members
only, preferably blue flowers or white flowers with blue ribbons,
these should be sent to the funeral directors.
   We hope you will understand that we can only invite family
members to our home after the funeral.

Once Ruth's body had been released, we knew she would be returned to the town where she had spent most of her life. Catherine had reconsidered and decided that she would like to see Ruth at the funeral directors. When I went in to see them to arrange this, they advised me that Ruth's body was by now not viewable. This surprised and shocked me, and I wondered what had happened in the intervening weeks, particularly after the second post-mortem. Why should her body have been invaded three times? I had seen for myself that the mortuary staff had taken great care. I was very distressed that the process that had permitted the second post-mortem and caused the long delay in arranging the funeral also denied Catherine her right to say goodbye to her sister.

Several family members wrote letters and sent photographs to put with Ruth in her coffin. She was wrapped in a bedspread that had been made for her by Vic's mother. My mother-in-law had nine grandchildren and she had crocheted a granny-squares bedspread for each grandchild soon after they were born. Ruth's had a blue border and she had always had it on her bed.

We had asked for family flowers only because it seemed such a pity for so many flowers to be left at the crematorium to die. We asked for blue or white flowers with blue ribbons because from a very early age Ruth loved the colour blue.

I went to a local florist to order a spray of blue and white flowers to be put on top of Ruth's coffin from Vic and myself. People ordering flowers for happy occasions surrounded me. They looked away, embarrassed, as the assistant passed me the cards for funerals. Tears poured unchecked and splashed onto the card as I wrote.

*

The morning of 13 March was grey and miserable. Somehow we got through the morning, setting the table and preparing food. Just before we stopped for lunch, I answered the door to find a man standing on the step with a huge, gaudy bouquet of flowers, stiffly arranged in florists' cellophane, saying that they were for the funeral. I asked him to take them to the funeral directors, but he was insistent that they were to be delivered to our address. I asked again that he take the flowers away, cringing at the lurid purples and oranges. He refused, and I retreated to the foot of our stairs and screamed, 'Take them away, take them away.' Vic rushed downstairs and took over. The deliveryman left, taking the flowers with him.

A few minutes later, the funeral directors telephoned to explain that my mother was in their office with some flowers she had picked from her garden to be put on the coffin. We had discussed our wishes with her and other family members and had agreed that just the flowers from Vic and me and from Catherine and Stephen would be on the coffin. I asked to speak to her and said that I was sorry but I had to say no, because Vic's mother and other family members might be upset if they saw that her flowers were on the coffin after what we had agreed. I was near to despair and wanted to tell her that I could have done without this request from her at such a time. I thought we had done everything we could to support her. I had telephoned her every day and seen her most days in the six weeks since Ruth died.

On arrival at the crematorium, we drove into the grounds and found that all the parking spaces were taken. We retreated and parked in a nearby lane. Walking up the drive, I remembered the last time we had been there, for my father's funeral. Ruth's ashes would be scattered to mingle with his in the lovely gardens, and so, in a way, they would be together again. I don't have any concept of a heaven where people who have died meet again; I wished that I did so I could think of Ruth being with her Grandad and other people she loved who had died.

As we drew close to the chapel, we saw a hearse drawing up in front and recognised the funeral director, so we knew that the coffin was Ruth's. My knees went weak, and we walked off into the wooded area for a few minutes, our arms around each other's waists, my head on Vic's shoulder.

On entering the chapel, we could see Ruth's coffin on a plinth at the front, two sprays of blue and white flowers, highlighted by a ray of sun from the windows, upon the light-brown wood of the coffin. A huge crowd of people were already seated.

Vic, Catherine, Stephen and I moved into the front row and the woman priest came forward to start the service.

> We are here to give thanks for the life and the love shared with
> Ruth over twenty-four years; to acknowledge the reality of
> her death and the distressing manner in which death came
> to her; to share some of the feelings we have about what has
> happened; and to commend her into God's care and love.

We had chosen well-known hymns. I was startled to hear a rich baritone singing with great clarity and vigour, and turned my head to see that it was the director of SENSE, one of the charities we had chosen to receive donations in memory of Ruth. His strength helped other people to sing the first hymn, 'Lead us, Heavenly Father, lead us'.

Catherine and I had had quite a task in selecting the excerpts from the letters and cards we had received, which by now totalled several hundred. We chose six that covered different periods of Ruth's life, and we decided that I would make a brief introduction and then we would read the excerpts in turn.

It was hard to do this, particularly as we had to stand up and face the assembly of mourning people. I read the first excerpt, from a letter from Paulene, a friend who had lodged with us while training to be a teacher in the late sixties:

> I remember a sunny, fair-haired, sturdy, little three-year-old – friendly, happy, full of life and affection – wriggling and chuckling as she was cuddled on your lap – asking one more time for Dr Seuss' *Green Eggs and Ham* or *The Cat in the Hat Came Back*. Independent, determined and very much her own person. Impossible not to love her. Those are just some of my memories. You, and everyone else she touched, will all have so many more.

Catherine completed the readings with a tribute from one of Ruth's trainees:

> When Ruth was my Training Officer she showed so much patience, common sense and good humour that it inspired us all to greater things.
> For many of us it was a second chance at being successful in life either at the difficult first steps of adult life or having the chance to try again after having a family.
> She helped us all to value ourselves and so be better able to help others.
> Although her life was regrettably so brief with so much potential, she had packed more into it than many people who reach seventy.

The service moved on to the painful moment when the curtains closed and concealed Ruth's coffin.

As the service ended, the woman priest beckoned us forward and showed us through a side door so that we could be the first to get outside and be ready to receive people as they left the chapel.

I wish I could remember all the people who were there, but I can't. There were hundreds of them, many we had never met before. Only nineteen months earlier, we had stood with

Catherine and Stephen and Ruth greeting the people who had shared the joy of Catherine and Stephen's wedding, and now here we were with a long line of sad people. Some were crying, some couldn't bring themselves to say anything, some hugged, some touched, some offered words of condolence.

The flowers had been laid in a group by the funeral directors, and the simplicity and freshness of the blue and white contrasted with the other collections outside the chapel. When we arrived home, I was very touched to see that the husband of one of my Cornish cousins was wearing a blue tie.

*

For many people, a funeral starts the process of adjusting to the loss of the person who has died, but it didn't feel like that for me. The police had told us that it would probably be a year before the trial would be held, and it would be some time before they would know the actual date. I noted that we would be told the date of the trial rather than being given any opportunity to say whether any timing would be more suitable for our needs.

It was now six weeks since Ruth's death. I felt as if I was in limbo. While Vic had returned to the job he had held for many years, my working life was less certain.

After leaving my work as director of SANDS at the beginning of 1989, I had embarked on freelance work. I continued to do the fundraising for SANDS for a year, and I became an associate consultant with Compass Partnership, which worked solely with charities and non-profit organisations. The clients I had been working with when Ruth died had all said that they preferred to wait for me to return, rather than be transferred to another consultant. I had already carried out interviews for some assignments, and more had to be done. I travelled to North Wales, to the Midlands, the North-East, unable to concentrate, frightened that I would lose control of myself, worried that I would be letting clients and my colleagues down. Travelling home from one visit, I saw a young woman with hair just like Ruth's getting into the carriage. I had to move into another carriage at the next station. At an adventure playground for children with disabilities someone called 'Ruth, Ruth, Ruth' to a child on a swing.

Someone asked how we were going to live the rest of our lives without Ruth. I responded by saying, 'Somehow we have to go on and not get bogged down in self-pity and bitterness.'

I felt I had three options – to get out, give in or go on. Getting out – committing suicide – did occur to me briefly as a way of escaping the pain. But I felt this wouldn't be the path to follow. Our family had a lot to cope with, and another death would take away Ruth's right to be mourned without distraction. To give in I saw as deciding to be miserable forever. This was very much at odds with Ruth's personality. I knew that if Ruth had lived and I had died, I would have wanted her to get on with her life and enjoy it; she would not have been impressed if we wallowed in despair.

I had learned a lot from working with bereaved parents at SANDS. The organisation saw its role as helping and supporting parents through their experience of bereavement so that they could gradually move towards the stage where they would be able to live the rest of their lives constructively, no longer defining themselves primarily as bereaved parents. The experience would always be part of their lives, but the hope was that it would not always dominate them. I hoped, but didn't feel confident, that eventually this would be possible for us, too.

Chapter Five
Towards the trial

MANY QUESTIONS still haunted me. Stephen repeated to us a conversation he had overheard when he went to the mortuary to identify Ruth, suggesting that drugs had played some part in her death. Through Ruth's friends we had also heard that Andrew Steel was a long-standing thief and drug user. He had often been to the house while Ruth was at work, without her knowledge.

I wrote to Geoff Parratt, the detective superintendent:

17th April 1990
It is now two-and-a-half months since Ruth died. My husband has said from the beginning that he does not want to know any details of her death. I feel differently about this and am aware that information is known both to the police officers involved in the case and to some of Ruth's friends which we have not been given.

I would be very grateful to know as much as possible as soon as possible. I realise that it is stressful for the police officers involved to give distressing information to murder victims' families but I am finding it harder to deal with grieving the loss of my daughter with an incomplete picture of what happened.

We would also both be grateful to know what effects of Ruth's the police are holding for evidence. We imagine that most of this is concerned with her work but we were upset on receiving her jewellery to find that the necklace she always wore was not returned to us with her rings and bracelet.

Geoff Parratt came to see me at home a week or so later with a female colleague. I was prepared with a list of questions:

—How did Andrew Steel get into the house?

—Did Ruth let him in?

—Did he have a key?

—Did he break in?

—Where in the house did Ruth die – we had noticed that a patch had been cut out of the bathroom flooring?

—Was she clothed?

—Where in her body was she stabbed/incised?

—Did the pathology report say how quickly she died?

—What time did he get to the house?

—Has he been committed for trial?

—Where will the trial be held?

—When we will have a date for the trial?

—How much notice will we be given of the trial date?

—What is the charge likely to be – murder, manslaughter?

—What is the plea likely to be – guilty, not guilty?

In response to this barrage, Geoff told me that they thought Andrew Steel had been at the house with Tom earlier in the day and had left the back door unlocked. Ruth died in her bedroom, and Andrew Steel had left blood-stained footprints in the bathroom, which is why the piece of flooring had been taken. He said, 'We think she must have died quickly, because one of the wounds went through her jugular vein.' I pressed for more information about the location and number of wounds, but he was, I felt, evasive and clearly uncomfortable in his responses about her injuries.

Tom's telephone call to the police had come at about midday, and they thought that Ruth had died between 3 and 6 a.m. The police would probably be given a date for the trial within the next few weeks: 'It could be early next year. Murder trials often take a year to come to court.' Geoff was convinced that the charge should be murder. The defence was likely to use Andrew Steel's drug-taking as the basis for a plea of manslaughter due to diminished responsibility. However, the fact that he had stolen and concealed some of Ruth's possessions – her credit card, cheque book, some cigarettes – and attempted to clean up the house and himself before leaving would, in Geoff's view, make such a plea difficult to substantiate.

We discussed the initial visit by the police, on 2 February, when we had been told that Ruth was dead. I explained that I had not been clear as to whether Ruth had committed suicide or been killed. He said that at that stage the police had not made a charge and therefore had to be very careful in their choice of words. He listened thoughtfully to what I had to say and said he would consider ways of ensuring that in future information about the cause of death could be given more explicitly.

At the end of the two-hour meeting, he said that he admired me for being strong where it was needed. I took this as quite a compliment from him, as we had agreed to differ on quite a number of issues.

*

I had already considered asking for a copy of the post-mortem report. I knew that I would want to attend the trial, and I didn't want to hear new information about Ruth's injuries for the first time in court. It riled me that people who had never known Ruth had this information while I didn't. I was also desperate for assurance that she had died quickly. Following the meeting with Geoff Parratt, I contacted a consultant pathologist I knew through my work at SANDS. She found out that I should be able to get a copy of the report by asking my GP to write to the coroner. I made an appointment with my

GP, who wrote the letter while I was in the surgery and gave it to me to post.

Vic and I went to the boat for a few days to move it to a new mooring. We had travelled on the canals together many times and made a good team, Vic steering and me operating the locks. The boat had been at Braunston in Oxfordshire while he was fitting it out; we were moving it to Sawley in Nottinghamshire. The spring days were grey, cold and damp, and we found it hard to be together in such a small space.

One evening we talked about what we could do to commemorate Ruth's life in ways that would honour her memory and her interests. Among her papers we had found an insurance policy she had taken out after she left home. This wasn't typical behaviour on her part; she did it to help a friend's brother, who had just started out as an agent. The policy included cover for her life, and we decided to use the money to form the basis of a small charitable trust.

Not long after the girls had started school, we had gone to the Isles of Scilly for our summer holiday, and then went every year until they were well into their teens. Over the years we had built up a number of traditions to enliven the long journey. I used to wrap up small presents so that they could open one every hundred miles. We always cheered when we crossed the Tamar into Cornwall. As we were usually travelling in early August, the game of completing the alphabet with all the car registrations entailed a particular thrill for the first one to spot a brand-new car.

One island, St Martin's, was a special favourite — even to the point where we had 'our beach' and got quite annoyed if other people arrived while we were there. In 1989, Vic and I met an artist on the islands and bought two prints of his watercolour paintings of St Martin's. We decided to ask if he would paint the view from the special beach for us. We would also order a wooden bench to be sited on St Martin's in Ruth's memory.

⋆

On our return from the boat, there was a big pile of mail waiting. I opened a brown envelope. It contained a Witness Order, which said:

> 24 April 1990
> YOU ARE HEREBY ORDERED (if notice is later given to you to that effect) to attend and give evidence at the trial of ANDREW STEEL at the CROWN COURT, sitting at (Central Criminal Court, Old Bailey, London E.C.) or at such other court as you may be directed.

This was quite a shock. I hadn't realised when I gave my statement in the week following Ruth's murder that it meant I could be called to give evidence at the trial. I looked at the piece of paper. Andrew Steel's name was prominent; Ruth's didn't even appear. It was as if she had never existed. There was no acknowledgement of our relationship. It could have been a document about a run-of-the-mill traffic offence in which I had no emotional involvement. There was no indication as to how long before the trial I would be notified if I had to give evidence. I shivered at the cold and distant nature of this document.

⋆

At the end of April, we heard good news from Catherine and Stephen. They were expecting their first baby at the end of the year. We knew that if either of our daughters had a family, their pregnancies would be complicated by the possibility that they might be carriers of the genetic disorder, Fragile X, that affected my brother. I wrote to a friend:

> *It will naturally be a time of a great mixture of feelings for all of us in*
> *combining mourning for Ruth while looking forward to a new life.*
> *There is the added anxiety about Fragile X but we are trying to be*
> *positive in that if neither Catherine or Ruth were affected it is more*
> *likely that I did not have the gene in recessed form and so it could not*
> *have been passed on to them. Catherine will be offered testing at eight-*
> *een weeks. It is confusing to feel such joy in the midst of such sadness*
> *but I am delighted at the prospect of the coming baby.*

I had gained a stone and a half in two-and-a-half months. I was also experiencing what might be the early signs of the onset of the menopause — or was it a physical response to grief? My temperature fluctuated, my head felt as if it was bursting with tension. I found that I couldn't laugh, even if I found something amusing, as instead of laughing, I cried. I had a persistent pain in my chest and the strain of trying not to cry caused tightness in my throat. I found that if I pressed the tip of my tongue hard against the back of my bottom teeth I could sometimes hold back tears, but I was still crying for extended periods each day. Somehow I managed to cry silently when I was at home, usually in the bath. I knew that Vic felt helpless when I cried and didn't know how to respond. He didn't talk about his own feelings and hardly mentioned Ruth. I was very worried about him, but he seemed to be coping in a way that suited him, keeping to his day-to-day routines. We were side by side, but not together, in our grief.

Early in May, Geoff Parratt phoned to say: 'The trial date has been set for Monday the fifteenth of October, but I have no idea about the plea so can't say how long the trial might take.' We had arranged many months before to go away with Catherine and Stephen on a camping holiday at the end of

September. By the time the trial started, Catherine would be well into her pregnancy and about to go on maternity leave. The date was about as good as it could be for us.

I didn't want to pressure Vic in any way, but made it clear that I wanted to attend the trial; I blocked off the last two weeks of October in my diary, taking on no work commitments then. Several friends offered to accompany me to court in turn if Vic decided not to attend.

*

My fiftieth birthday was at the beginning of June, and originally I had planned to hold a party. Instead, Catherine, Stephen and my mother came to share a meal with us, and they gave me an original oil painting of a bluebell wood. It had been my mother's idea, and the whole family had clubbed together to give me this special gift. I have always loved bluebell woods, and had a picture of some in my bedroom when I was a child that stimulated many fantasy stories. Ruth had been very involved in the planning and had taken my mother to see the artist. I wanted to show that I was pleased, but the poignancy of the shimmering blue, Ruth's favourite colour, made it hard.

Weeks had now gone by since our GP had written to ask for a copy of the post-mortem report. When he phoned in July, he sounded embarrassed: 'I've received a letter saying that I can't have a copy.' Neither he nor I could understand why he had been refused. He had been Ruth's GP for most of her life, though she had transferred to another practice when she moved to Enfield.

I decided to write directly to the coroner.

24th July 1990
My General Practitioner wrote at my request in May, asking for a

copy of the post-mortem report on my daughter, Ruth Moreland, who died on February 2nd. A man is held in custody having been charged with her murder. My G P has advised me that he has been told that a copy of the report cannot be sent to him.

I am now writing to you to request that a copy of the post-mortem report be made available to me, either directly or through my G P, for the following reasons:

—— I have been advised that I may be required as a witness at the trial which will start on the 15th October at the Old Bailey. I do not wish to hear details of Ruth's injuries for the first time in a situation which will naturally be stressful for me.

—— Even if I am not required as a witness I would be in the position of hearing this information in public or never hearing it if I decide not to attend.

—— The factual information I have at present is contained in your interim certificate which gives the cause of Ruth's death as 'Haemorrhage due to multiple stab wounds and incisions'. Nothing will restore Ruth's life but I am finding that my grieving for her is being hampered without information on the extent of her injuries.

My understanding of the law regarding access to the post-mortem report is that this lies within your discretion. I do feel that I am a 'properly interested person' and would appreciate your help. If it is not possible for me to have this information I would appreciate being given a sound, legal reason for such a decision.

The problems I was encountering in getting the information I wanted made me feel that I needed to understand more about the processes involved in a trial. Although I am an omnivorous reader, I had rarely read murder mysteries or accounts of real-life crimes. I had a very rough idea of how trials were conducted, but had no direct experience of being in a court during the trial of a serious crime.

I talked again to my magistrate friend. We had known each other since her daughter and Ruth were babies in prams; they were born one day after each other. She arranged for me to meet a court official who had agreed go through the usual sequence of events of a murder trial with me. I would also be able to sit in a court during a case with a jury so that I could begin to understand how the trial in October would be conducted.

We travelled on 27 July to Southwark Crown Court, where my friend was sitting in an appeal court with a judge. We went to the magistrates' retiring room and talked about the draft of an article I'd been sent by the information officer at Victim Support. It was about the role of their volunteers in supporting the families of murder victims during and after the trial. The title of the article was 'The Unkind Funeral'; it had alerted me to the possibility that there would be no opportunity to make any rebuttal if the defence said untrue or derogatory things about Ruth.

While we were talking, another magistrate, a tall, elegant lady, arrived and overheard part of our conversation. After putting some things into a small locker, she turned and said, 'Could I see the article, please?' After glancing through it she looked at me and said, 'My son was murdered five years ago.' I told her why I had come to the court. We stared intently at each other for a few moments and then she said, 'I learned a lot from my experience and would like to help you.' She was due to go into the court for the same session as my friend, so we only had a few minutes to talk. She told me she would write to me to share more information. She said she and her husband had sat within the court during the trial of her son's killers, rather than in the public gallery. This possibility hadn't occurred to me.

My friend took me to the court official's room and left to go to the appeal court.

Vic had asked me to find out if it would be possible to obtain a copy of the trial proceedings. The answer was that although evidence was taken down in shorthand, it was unusual for the notes to be transcribed. Someone with a recognised interest in the case could ask for a transcript to be made, but this would cost several thousand pounds. This answer eliminated that option; we didn't have the money to pay the fee.

I asked the court official about the witness statement I had made in February and the notice I had received saying that I could be called to give evidence. How soon would I know if I would have to do this, and how would that affect my attendance at the rest of the trial? I was told that the police would advise me as soon as the prosecution and defence counsels had listed their witness requirements; this might be very close to the trial date. I would not be allowed to enter the court until I had given evidence. If it was possible that I might be recalled, I wouldn't be able to re-enter the court. I was torn between fury at having been asked to give such a statement without being advised that this could be the outcome, and knowing that, at the time, I would have agreed to do anything to help Matt, who had done so much for us. Still, I might have asked somebody else to make the statement if I had known that doing so could jeopardise my attending the trial.

The official carefully went through the stages of a trial with the charge of murder and said it was possible that the plea might be to a lesser crime than the charge – that is, the charge could be murder, but the defendant might plead guilty to manslaughter. If this was the case, both counsels would have a discussion with the judge in his chambers before the trial began. The prosecution's task was to establish proof of guilt; the defence would challenge the prosecution case. Witnesses to support prosecution and defence would be called to give evidence. At the end of the trial, the prosecution would sum up first and then the defence. The judge would summarise the evidence and advise the jury on any points of law. The jury would then retire to consider their verdict. The court official thought that as the trial was likely to take place at the Old Bailey, an experienced judge would be in charge.

If the verdict was murder, then a life sentence would be automatically passed, and the judge would send a recommendation about the number of years to be served to the Home Office for a minister to consider. If the verdict was manslaughter, the judge would announce the sentence and the prison term to be served at the end of the trial.

I then sat in a court listening to a case about a burglary. It was difficult to concentrate. I was reflecting on the extraordinary coincidence of meeting someone at the court whose son had been murdered, and also trying to absorb all the information I had been given by the court official.

The magistrate wrote to me within days, sending four closely typed pages packed with vital information for me. She set out the reasons why she and her husband had attended the trial of the men who had killed their son. First, it was so that they could hear, for the first time, exactly what had happened and, as far as possible, why it had happened. Second, to see for themselves that the people who had murdered their son were not monsters, but ordinary people who had acted in an extraordinary manner. Finally, they wanted to be there to honour the memory of their son.

She was insistent on the importance of both parents being present, and any other family members who wished to attend. Her husband had initially been reluctant, and many of their friends had tried to persuade them both not to attend, but in the end they did go together.

They had a friend in the legal profession who was able to intervene on their behalf to get seating within the court. She wrote:

> *The public gallery is crammed with relations of the accused, relations of witnesses and all sorts of other people, such as people writing books about trials, or planning TV serials (both were there when our sons were in the gallery and of course their view of the evidence etc. was not always very pleasant to hear).*

She confirmed what I had been suspecting for a long time: that as the parents of the victim, we had no legal rights. Some defence counsels would turn anything possible to their advantage, and anyone's life could be presented in a damning light. She advised me to prepare a statement about Ruth's life which, if necessary, could be given to the press.

They hadn't attended the last day of the trial, because they wanted to avoid the press, and also because she didn't want to see someone given a life sentence and perhaps be thought by his relations to be gloating.

She closed her letter by offering to help, if she could, with any problems we might have in getting seating within the court.

★

The following week, the post-mortem report arrived. I didn't open it, but phoned to make an appointment to see our GP so that he could read it through and explain any clinical terms that I might not understand. The receptionist fitted me in for an appointment in the late morning. After reading through the report, the GP shook his head slowly and said sombrely, 'You will understand it only too well. I advise you to choose a day when little else is happening to read it.' He had known Ruth since she was a baby.

In the afternoon, I went with Catherine to the hospital where she was having an 'ordinary' scan done – to check that the baby was all present and correct and to confirm the expected date of delivery. The radiologist was pleasant enough, but not enthusiastic about Catherine being accompanied by me for the scan. It was just another pregnancy, no doubt, for her, but to us the baby would be very special. It had been difficult to feel the natural pleasure at the thought of the coming new life, not to replace Ruth in any way, but as a positive event to look forward to. Catherine had had an earlier scan at Guy's Hospital and tests to see if Fragile X were present, and this had shown clearly that the baby was male. There would be a delay of some weeks before the results were known.

To see him on the screen, with little waving hands, heart beating vigorously, his whole skeleton outlined, the major internal organs already identifiable, suddenly brought home even more strongly the appalling dilemma that Catherine and Stephen would face if he was affected by Fragile X.

When I got home, I opened the envelope containing the post-mortem report. There was no accompanying letter offering any explanation as to why I had received it now. The report confirmed my worst fears – hardly any part of Ruth's body had escaped being wounded. I was surprised to see that eight people were present during the examination, even though it took place at 11.30 p.m. on the day that Ruth died. The list of injuries took up seven pages, recording nearly a hundred 'stab and incised wounds, plus grazes and bruises, all received within a short time prior to her death'.

The final paragraph summed up:

> The injuries she has received have been multiple and forceful
> and have damaged vital structures with fatal blood loss. The large,
> gaping, blackened wound across the front of the neck has com-
> pletely divided the windpipe (trachea) and oesophagus. The maxi-
> mum dimensions of this horizontal wound were 11cms wide by
> 7cms deep. The neck muscles had been divided, and the main
> artery and vein on the right hand side of the neck.

This was the major wound that caused Ruth's death. Certainly this injury alone would be incompatible with life – breathing would be impossible, the circulation of blood would have stopped moving both towards and away from her heart.

I took a ruler and measured 11 centimetres across my neck and tried to imagine a knife being pushed in for 7 centimetres. I shuddered at the hatred, the lack of control that must have lain behind this savage attack. The level of violence and the number of injuries indicated that Ruth had been the focus for a great deal of long-standing pent-up anger.

Although I was very shocked at the extent and severity of her injuries, I was still relieved to have the detailed informa-tion. It meant that I knew what to expect during the trial. I could understand now why she had been almost fully cov-ered at the mortuary, and why her head had been in such a strange position.

However, it didn't relieve the still regular nightmares about how long it took for Ruth to die and how much she had suffered. It wasn't clear from the report in what order the wounds had been inflicted, and her neighbour had heard her screaming. I knew that Ruth had suffered, and the frequent nightmares continued. Images of her terror and helplessness with no protection from her attacker, her lying there with so many terrible wounds, alone and without comfort, pursued me relentlessly. I would go to sleep, but then wake up trembling and unable to get back to sleep. I would try to pass the time until daybreak by sitting alone downstairs, listening to the Rutter *Requiem* that Ruth's teacher had given us and reading.

*

Geoff Parratt, the detective superintendent, telephoned to ask how we were, and sounded shocked to hear that I had managed to get a copy of the post-mortem report. He had phoned to tell me that he would be meeting the defence lawyers the following week, and he understood a large part of their case would revolve around Andrew Steel's use of drugs, including LSD. I asked him if any tests had been done on Ruth for the presence of drugs, as this was not mentioned in the post-mortem report. I didn't think she had taken drugs, but I wanted to be certain that this had been checked in case the defence tried to imply that she was a drug user. He said that this had been done, and no drugs were found in Ruth's body. He also confirmed that the trial would be held at the Old Bailey.

Following the meetings with the Southwark court official and the magistrate whose son had been murdered, I decided to visit the Old Bailey so that when I attended the trial I would have some idea of the physical layout of the building and its atmosphere. My magistrate friend again offered to accompany me. I was delighted when Vic said quite suddenly, as he left for work one day the week before the visit, that he thought he would 'tag along'. It was an encouraging sign that he wanted to see the Old Bailey, but I didn't assume that this meant he had decided to attend the trial.

We went to the public gallery and heard the summing-up of a case concerned with a charge of robbing a shop. This was in one of the newer courts – the original ones were closed for redecoration. When the case finished, the three of us went to a nearby café to have a sandwich and a cup of tea, then Vic went back to work.

My friend and I went back to the Old Bailey to see if we could find a case that was just starting, so that I could see a jury being sworn in. The court officials were very off-putting when we asked for their help. They insisted that we waited on the landing, and said they would let us know if a case was about to start. I was somewhat taken aback when one of them put his head around the door and said that there was a case already under way which we would find interesting – it was a buggery case. I said with as much dignity as I could muster that it was the process rather than the content that I was interested in, and we wanted to wait for the start of a case. I was conscious that if Ruth had been with me, we would have been doubled up with laughter at this encounter.

After a long wait, a case was due to start and we walked along the narrow corridor to the public gallery. There was a technical hitch as the court needed further information, so the jury was not sworn in and the case was adjourned. However, the delay enabled me to have a conversation with the usher in the public gallery, who confirmed that it was possible to arrange seating in the body of the court at a trial. Having sat in the public gallery for a brief time in two courts, I was even keener not to have to do that during the trial relating to Ruth's murder. I didn't want to encounter Andrew Steel's family and friends, for their sake as well as mine. I didn't want to hear what tourists and other casual attenders thought about the proceedings. I had also realised that there could be a risk of not being able to get seating in the public gallery, as the policy was, 'first come, first served'.

★

In the middle of August, the results of the tests on Catherine and Stephen's baby finally came through indicating that their son was not affected by Fragile X. A blood sample had been taken from the umbilical cord, and the geneticist said that the test was 100 per cent accurate. It was such a relief for them not to have to face decisions about terminating the pregnancy, particularly as Catherine had already felt the baby moving.

*

Matt Miller, the detective sergeant, had kept in touch, and had always said that I should contact him at any time if there was anything more he could do to help. I phoned him and asked if he could come to see me to discuss the post-mortem report. It would also be an opportunity to ask him if he had any more information he could share with me.

It had been some time since I had seen Matt. I asked him what had been happening in his life. Modestly, he said, 'I've been commended for arresting four armed robbers.' He'd also moved house, and his wife was expecting another baby. We talked about the post-mortem report and about the hours prior to Ruth's death.

Matt said, 'Andrew Steel had been with Tom and two girls, who also knew Ruth, Claire and Libby, who lived in Palmers Green. Some of the talk had been about Ruth and someone said something to the effect that it would be a good thing if Ruth were not around any more.' I knew that Claire and Ruth had been through good and bad times together. They had gone to social events together, but there had been a major falling-out some years before when Claire went out with one of Ruth's boyfriends.

'Later that evening,' Matt went on, 'Andrew Steel approached Libby for sex and was rejected. When he got to the house,

Ruth had come downstairs – whether to let him in or because she heard the noise of him entering was not clear. There was a fight in the kitchen and she hit him – probably with a saucepan. She must then have run upstairs to get away from him, as most of the attack took place there.' Matt believed that 'Ruth died defending her integrity'. His theory was that Andrew Steel, having been frustrated earlier in the evening, wanted to have sex with Ruth, and when she also rejected him, he attacked her.

Matt had interviewed most of the potential witnesses, and said he felt he almost knew Ruth. Late in 1989, she had been filmed at work as part of a training video. We had been sent a copy of the finished video and the out-takes that featured Ruth. I asked Matt if he would like to see it; he was keen, but anxious in case watching it might distress me. After seeing it, he was quite upset, saying, 'She was just so full of life,' and 'What a waste.' He took a copy to show his colleagues at the station.

He offered to ask if I might not be called as a witness, so that my attendance at court would not be prejudiced, and said he would also ask about arranging seating for at least two people in the body of the court.

That evening we had a meal with Catherine, Stephen and my mother at our home to celebrate Mum's and Stephen's recent birthdays.

I got through the meal, but once they had gone home, I retreated to the bath and cried and cried, drained by the effort of taking in the information learned from Matt in the afternoon.

Mainly, I found it was smaller things that made me cry: finding Ruth's school name tapes; coming across an old birthday card from her to me; someone using the word ruthless. That evening was a real low point.

*

In the autumn of 1989, Vic had pruned the pyracantha hedge which screens the shed in our garden. It hadn't been cut back for a long time, so some of the branches were very large and there was a considerable quantity. Over the winter and through the spring, they had been frozen and wet and then baked throughout the very hot summer of 1990.

I decided to spend half an hour each day cutting the branches up into small pieces and putting them into bags to take to the dump. I needed to use long-armed loppers to get through the tough wood. As I did this, a lot of aggression surfaced, and I thought a lot about Andrew Steel. I didn't know him, but I hated what he had done. Would it be any help to see him at the trial? Would I hate him then? Was he suffering? Did he realise what he had done?

Chapter Six
A setback

THE TRIAL was now approaching quickly. Vic, much to my relief, had decided that he would attend, so I didn't need to take up any of the many offers from family and friends to accompany me if he decided not to come. Geoff Parratt phoned to say that he would do his best to get us seats in the court, but it was the judge taking the case who would make the decision. Some judges were reluctant to give permission, as they had had bad experiences with the court being disrupted by relatives.

Geoff also said that he had heard unofficially that the medical and forensic facts of the case would not be disputed. The defence would revolve around Andrew Steel's use of drugs. If that were so, the defence would be likely to seek a lesser charge, of manslaughter. I hadn't heard from anyone about being called as a witness. I decided not to ask, afraid that by doing so I might jeopardise my being able to be in the court throughout the trial.

Then, on 5 October, Geoff phoned again to break the news that the trial, which should have started on 15 October, was to be deferred until 21 January. The reason given was that the original defence counsel could no longer present the defence, and the counsel appointed to take over would not have sufficient time to study the brief. Geoff said that if the trial had gone ahead on the due date, it might have left open the possibility for an appeal on the grounds that the defence had not been well prepared.

This delay was an awful blow. In January, Catherine's baby

son would just have been born, and I wanted to be available to be with her if she wanted help. I couldn't tear myself in two to be both with her and at the trial: how could I choose between my daughters? The other awful prospect was that if the trial went into a second week, we might be in court on the anniversary of Ruth's death. We had been told by Geoff very early on that murder trials can take up to a year to come to court, and it is not uncommon for them to take place around the anniversary of the death, but we had hoped to be spared that.

I had deliberately not taken on any new work assignments for October, and therefore had more time to brood and talk to friends and family members. There was considerable speculation as to why the defence counsel had pulled out. One of Ruth's uncles said, 'They couldn't bring themselves to defend the little shit,' and someone with a cynical turn of mind said, 'Something that paid better came up.' I felt sorry for Geoff having to break the news to us.

For some time we had been considering redesigning our front garden. I hired a skip to be delivered on the Friday before the trial should have taken place. At the weekend, Vic and I knocked down the walls that surrounded the garden — they were about a foot high. Swinging the sledgehammer with considerable force released a lot of tension in a productive way. I hurled chunks of stone and plaster into the skip, relishing the sound as they landed. Our elderly neighbour came out to register his concern that I might damage myself, exerting such vigour, and was surprised to be told that I was enjoying myself.

Despite this outlet, the setback caused by the postponement of the trial date affected my struggle to maintain stability, and the separation between my public and private faces was crumbling. The means I had used to maintain control when in public were no longer working. Telling myself that adults don't cry in public didn't help any more. Trying to keep cheerful for Ruth's sake seemed pointless. The circle of family and friends whose ears and shoulders I had used liberally during the preceding months were, I felt, getting weary — and they, too, were bearing their own sorrow over Ruth's death.

I had tried hard not to establish 'no-go' areas — such as avoiding eating foods that Ruth enjoyed, or not going to places that had particular associations with her — but this boundary collapsed. Anything that reminded me of her or roused my emotions quickly resulted in tears. I dreaded going to sleep, as I would dream vividly about Ruth, then have to wake and face all over again the knowledge that she was dead.

*

Victim Support sent me an invitation to their Annual General Meeting, held at the end of October. The Lord Chancellor, Lord Mackay of Clashfern, was to be the main speaker. During his presentation, he touched on the issue of seating in court:

> Cases where a death is involved, whether by murder, manslaughter, or causing death by reckless driving can be particularly sensitive. Such cases, coupled with sexual offences on children, and rape, are perhaps the most emotionally charged cases that come before the higher courts and inevitably they are also frequently the cases that attract wide press and public interest.
>
> I mentioned earlier the need for public confidence in the courts. Access by the press and public generally are factors crucial to justice being seen to be done and this can on occasions conflict with the legitimate wishes of families of victims

to be present. Offering unlimited access to relatives and identifying reserved seats for victims and their families is difficult on a practical level.

Relatives of victims may wish to consider whether specific seat reservation, where courts can provide it, is desirable in that it may well draw attention to them. I have however asked the courts to try to assist the families of both defendants and victims whenever possible if requests for reserved seats are received in particular cases. Courts will usually have the capacity to accommodate at least one near relative (usually a parent or partner makes the request) without the need to make specific arrangements.

I couldn't attract the attention of the chairman to say something during the question-and-answer session that followed. I waited a couple of weeks, thinking over what I had heard, and decided to write to the Lord Chancellor to express my reactions to his statement about seating in court. After setting out the background to my concerns, I wrote:

> I am sure you will understand that the trial will be a very stressful and significant event in our lives. I find it hard to understand why seating in the court for the victim's family depends on the decision of an individual. I quite appreciate that some judges may have had the experience of proceedings being disrupted by relatives and so may be wary of granting such seating; but feel this problem could be dealt by relatives being informed very clearly that if they create any disturbance they will have to leave the court immediately and will not be allowed to return.
>
> During your speech you made a comment to the effect that families might like to consider the possibility that they may be more vulnerable to identification if seated within the court. Having given the matter careful consideration during this year and having visited two courts to sit in the public gallery while cases were in session, I would like to share with you the reasons why the alternative of sitting in the public gallery is even less acceptable to me:

— I do not want to hear the comments of people not directly involved in the proceedings.

— I do not want to run the risk of not being able to obtain seats because members of the general public have already taken the available seating.

— I do not want to sit next to members of the defendant's family during the proceedings.

I fully accept that the defendant's family may have very similar reasons for wanting seats within the court and that if both the victim's and the defendant's families request seating this presents a further dilemma for the court officials.

Finally, while accepting the practical difficulties of arranging seating within the court for the families, I hope very much that we and others would not be faced with the decision to be made if only one seat were made available. The majority of parents in our circumstances would wish to be together to offer mutual support and those attending without a partner are likely to need and welcome a support of their choice.

By now, the trial should have been behind us, but we still had a long wait to endure, in parallel with waiting for the birth of our first grandchild. I had worked in the voluntary sector for many years and so I knew many people who worked in bereavement charities. This made me very inhibited about approaching any of these charities for help.

I phoned the Samaritans. Not because I felt suicidal, but because I needed to talk to someone who was not emotionally involved. The man who answered was calm and sympathetic. He suggested that I might like to call in at one of the Samaritan centres. I did this, and subsequently saw the same woman several times during the final part of the year. It was an interesting experience on a number of levels. The Samaritans' approach was far more directional than I had expected.

The woman I saw made suggestions and offered practical help. I mentioned that Vic had been unable to discuss the post-mortem report with me after reading it. She immediately suggested that I brought it with me next time so that she could read it, too, and then discuss it with me if I wanted to do this. I was quite nervous about it, as the contents of the document are so horrific, but it was a great relief to talk about it to someone who didn't know Ruth.

The Samaritan made a really helpful comment after our discussion about the post-mortem report: 'Ruth died once; you don't have to keep on experiencing her death over and over again.' This was just what I had been doing, and so I was finding it impossible to move forward from the moment of her death. It was a real turning point for me; I got off the treadmill and accepted that it wasn't helping Ruth or me. I couldn't do anything to help Ruth now, and could have done nothing to prevent her death.

Chapter Seven
A new friend

IN 1988, I HAD WATCHED a programme called *Fourteen Days in May* about Death Row in the United States. As a child, I was shocked when the news emerged that Timothy Evans had been executed for murders committed by John Christie. This made me think about capital punishment, and I came to the conclusion that if killing another human being was wrong, then killing someone convicted of murder was also wrong.

I had been aware of the situation in America, where only some states impose the death penalty; where the majority of the 3,000 prisoners on Death Row are likely to be poor and black, and many of them would be imprisoned for years in awful conditions before the death sentence was carried out. The programme brought the facts into human form by featuring four of the Death Row prisoners.

Jan Arriens, a Quaker who lived in Cambridge, also saw *Fourteen Days in May*. He wrote to the men featured in the programme, and thus started on the path which led to him founding an organisation called LifeLines.

Towards the end of 1990, I saw a brief article in *The Friend*, a Quaker publication, describing LifeLines and its appeal for more people to come forward to befriend prisoners on Death Row through writing letters. I considered whether I should do this. I could see that it would be a practical way of helping someone who wanted friendship. It would also give me the opportunity get to know as a human being someone who had committed a murder. I thought it might help me in my efforts to keep a separation between Andrew Steel as a whole person and what he had done.

But Jan Arriens might not think I was a suitable person for a prisoner to correspond with. I wrote to Jan, explaining that Ruth had been murdered earlier in the year and that we were still waiting for the trial to be held. I would understand if he felt that it wouldn't be possible for him to put me in touch with a Death Row prisoner.

He responded quickly:

17th December 1990

In the three years I have been swept up in the correspondence with prisoners on Death Row, few things have affected me as much as your letter. I can only hope that your decision to write to someone in the United States will be as healing as it is courageous.

I am enclosing a letter I have received from a man in Texas, Micheal Richard, asking for a pen friend. It is an unusually well written letter that should provide the basis for a worthwhile correspondence. Micheal is black, born 24 August 1959. He has been on Death Row since 4 September 1987.

Micheal's undated letter was written on one side of flimsy lined paper with a double red margin line to the left. The paper was punched with two holes for filing.

I found his writing difficult to read and had to make several attempts to decipher all the words:

Greeting Friend

My name is Micheal W. Richard and I am a death-sentenced prisoner in the state of Texas. While there has been changes for the better recently on death row, I'm still contained in my cell for 21 hours a day, with exception to the 15 minutes I get to take a shower.

My reason for writing your organisation is to ascertain if I could possibly get someone to correspond with me. Needless to say being

locked up for so many hours each day of my life, loneliness is a
constant companion.

I really do need someone on the outside to communicate with so that
I can maintain my mental balance.

If it is possible I would like to communicate with a very mature and
open minded woman, your assistance would be greatly appreciated.

I understand that your organization sometimes helps prisoners on
'Death Row' to find a pen-pal, I hope that you will be able to help me.

Thank you for your precious time, and I pray that you will be able
to help me to find a Friend. I hope to hear from someone soon.

But if you can't find anyone, please put my name and number in the
newspaper!!!

It was very close to Christmas when I wrote to Micheal for
the first time, too close to send him a Christmas card, but I
sent a calendar with my letter. It probably wasn't the most
sensitive gift to someone whose life was measured in days
spent in isolation and whose time left on earth was uncertain.

I wasn't sure what his expectations of a 'very mature and
open minded woman' would be. In terms of my age, I was
certainly mature. In my first letter, I told him something
about my life and about Ruth's death and that we were waiting for the trial, which would start on 21 January. If he didn't
want to start corresponding with me, Jan could put him in
touch with someone else. If he did want us to correspond, I
would make a commitment to write to him once a month.

In his reply, he described himself as being in very good
physical health, at 5 feet 9 inches in height and weighing 154
pounds.

My skin colour is a very light brown and brown eyes, black hair, most of
my friends called me 'Louisiana Red' because I'm from Louisiana and

not Texas. My birthplace is the capital of Louisiana which is Baton Rouge but I grew up in a small town in Texas called Hockley.

He offered his condolences on Ruth's death and told me that he had also suffered the murder of a family member: 'My mother was murdered over six months ago, and I still find myself writing to her, because I know that she would try to understand my pain that I must endure each day and would love and accept me just as I am.'

He went on:

I want to be more than a pen-pal to you, I want us to be supportive and caring with our hearts open and honest . . . to me it would be senseless and serve no purpose to write to each other if we can't share our feelings.

A friendship based on understanding, respect, trust and consideration is one that will endure any challenge that occurs in life and I feel if we don't try to establish this type of friendship we would just be word processing letters to each other from afar.

Lesley, there's no way a man in my situation could be contained under these circumstances and not have some severe needs.

But my deepest and ultimate need is to be loved and cared about, sometimes my heart hurts so badly until I just sit and cry, I'm tired and hurting and being alone and tired of shallow and insensitive people.

He asked if I could send some photographs of family members and myself and of our garden. 'I haven't seen any flowers or shrubs in over six years now and I only get to see the sky through a small window, so I spend most of my time reading or drawing. I love to sing and listen to music, mainly Burl Ives or something romantic!!! Smile!'

And so our correspondence began, and gradually I learned more about this complex man on the other side of the world, who came from a very different background to mine and who surprised me with his ability to remain sane and even to be jocular. One letter finished with the salutation: 'Well my dear friend, the time has come for me to do like a gentleman with a rose and tip my hat and bring this letter to a close.'

Chapter Eight
The trial

REFLECTING on the events of 1990, I considered the differences between the misery caused through mental illness and that which arises in response to a specific event. Following Catherine's birth in 1964, I had suffered a manic-depressive illness which returned on a cyclical basis over many years. My reactions to Ruth's murder and to my illness were both painful. However, the mental illness was more frightening because there was no identifiable reason for the despairing feelings. Each time it happened, I didn't know if I would recover, and there was the ever-present fear that the illness might return. At least now I knew *why* I was suffering.

I had heard Jim Swire, whose daughter Flora died in the plane that exploded over Lockerbie in 1989, quote Aristotle. Aristotle said that he felt that there was one loss from which a person could never recover: the loss of a child. It struck too deeply, he thought, at the foundations of a life for there ever to be a chance of rebuilding.

I hoped this wouldn't be true for Vic and myself. It wouldn't be much of a tribute to Ruth to spend the rest of our lives grieving.

Nineteen ninety had been the hardest year of my life, and maintaining the energy needed to keep going with daily tasks, let alone anything that presented a challenge, required great effort. Grieving is very hard work, and the way in which I'd had to struggle to obtain the information I wanted had drained me even further.

Vic and I had now had many years of relative comfort

financially, when day-to-day expenses could be afforded without really thinking about them. This was a great change for us; we had both come from economically deprived backgrounds, and we had been hard up during the early years of our marriage. The aftermath of Ruth's death had meant that there were long periods when I couldn't work. The build-up of costs associated with her death – for example, our telephone bills were far higher than they had ever been – meant that before the end of 1990, my savings were exhausted and my income was severely reduced. I'm not sure that I could have coped with a full-time job, but my plans to earn my living by working freelance had been severely damaged.

Vic and I have always had a very comfortable relationship over money, dividing up the areas for which we took personal responsibility according to our individual incomes. It had been a long time since I had needed to draw on his earnings. But now, because I had put on weight, I needed to buy some new clothes. Although I knew that Vic would say 'How much do you want?' and immediately make the money available, I resented this further impact of Ruth's murder on our lives. I had been financially independent for many years; now this, too, had been taken away from me.

I went into London for a meeting, and on the way home had to wait for a train at King's Cross. I looked for a magazine to read on the way home. The book area in WHSmith was divided into sections with labels along the top of the shelves. In the one headed 'Crime', the word 'murder' leapt out at me from the covers of the books. I had to restrain myself from wrenching the books from the shelves and stamping on them. How dare people enjoy reading them, and how dare people earn money from such human misery?

⋆

The New Year had opened without the birth of our grandson. Each day we hoped to hear that he was on his way. He was finally born on 7 January. Vic and I went to the hospital early in the evening. Seeing Christopher cradled in Catherine's arms, she looking wan and tired after a long stop-start labour, was a magical moment. I had hand-knitted him a shawl and a very small matinée jacket. Catherine put aside the hospital blanket and dressed Christopher in his new jacket, folded him snugly in the shawl and handed him to me.

After Catherine came home from hospital, I went to be with her for part of each day over the next two weeks. I thought pram pushing was like typing or cycling: that once you had mastered it, you didn't lose the knack. It wasn't so. Their pram was a modern one with swivel wheels which seemed to have a mind of their own, and I had forgotten whether it was better to put the front or the back wheels down first when negotiating kerbs. Walking Christopher around his home village in the crisp winter days was very enjoyable for me and gave Catherine a chance to rest quietly.

I wanted to continue to be available for Catherine, yet I also wanted to attend the trial. I couldn't bear the thought that people might think that Ruth's family cared so little for her that they wouldn't bother to be there. It felt like the last thing I would ever be able to do for her. Catherine said she understood that we needed to go the Old Bailey; Stephen's mother offered to come and stay with her during the trial so that she would not be alone during the day.

I thought about what to wear to the Old Bailey. What is appropriate dress for such an occasion? Would black be best? Bright colours didn't seem to be right. In the end, I bought a cheap navy skirt and two dark-coloured tops. I knew that I would want to get rid of the clothes when the trial had finished.

I wondered whether there might be another last-minute cancellation. It was a relief when Geoff Parratt phoned to say that he would meet us at the front door of the Old Bailey half an hour before the trial was due to start on 21 January. Seating had been arranged for us within the court, and he would take us through the security entrance. Geoff let us know that the charge would be murder and the likely plea would be guilty of manslaughter. He said that he had been told that Andrew Steel would not be giving evidence, on the advice of his counsel.

First day of the trial, Monday 21 January 1991
The train pulled into Moorgate station and Vic and I emerged into a bitterly cold day with a keen wind blowing across the High Walk pedestrian path as we walked over London Wall to the Old Bailey.

On the outside wall, a notice listed the trials being held that day, giving the name of the defendants and the judges and the number of the court. With dismay, I saw that the trial of Andrew Steel would be held in Court No.1. This court had witnessed many high-profile trials over the years. It was the court most likely to attract media interest.

Geoff met us and took us into the reception area, then had to leave to meet prosecution witnesses. The receptionist called the official who would conduct us to the court. On the way through the imposing building with its lofty, highly decorated ceilings, he lectured us as if we were recalcitrant adolescents, rather than a staid, middle-aged couple. 'You must not speak or attract attention to yourselves in any way during the trial. If you do, you will be ejected immediately and not allowed to return. You are being given a great privilege in being allowed to sit in the court; it isn't usual.' We were going into completely new territory, embarking on the ordeal of sitting through the trial, hoping for and yet also fearing the information that would be revealed.

We were shown into the empty court. It was a large cavern, the lower walls lined with dark wooden panels. There was seating at several levels. We were shown to an area behind the large dock, in which Andrew Steel would be on view during the trial. The wooden seating was tiered; we chose to sit at the highest level so that we could see as much of the court as possible. The public gallery was off to our right, high above us. At the front of the court, the jury seats were at a lower level to our left. Down in the well of the court, there were desks and tables piled high with papers and a separate desk with equipment for the stenographer; the judge's bench loomed above the court, bathed in a cold light from the glass cupola above.

Gradually, people entered the well of the court and took up their places to start what for them was just another working day. Quiet conversations were held. More papers and books were set out on the tables.

The public gallery filled with people, including two of our nieces. I wondered if any of Andrew Steel's family were there or elsewhere in the court – there was no one sitting near us. In fact, we were isolated in an area that could easily have seated over a hundred people. A police officer we hadn't met before came and introduced himself as George and told us who would be giving evidence that day.

The people who had been called for jury service were brought in. As there were no objections from the defence or prosecution counsels, they were quickly sworn in. They were a mixture, just as we had hoped, with people of both sexes, of different ages and ethnic groups.

A court official asked everyone to stand for the entry of the judge. Quite suddenly, Andrew Steel appeared in the defendant's box between two warders. I caught only a quick glimpse of the side of his face as he walked up the steps from the cells, and soon I could only see the back of his head. He glanced up towards the public gallery and was acknowledged by some people sitting there, so I assumed they were members of his family or his friends.

I wanted to look at him closely – this was the first time I had seen him. Because he was above us, it wasn't possible to gauge his height, but he was a sturdily built man. His shoulders were held stiffly; his head was bowed. He confirmed his name and answered 'Not guilty' to the charge of murder. He pleaded guilty to manslaughter due to diminished responsibility.

I felt too awed by the surroundings and intimidated by the lecture on not drawing attention to ourselves to show any reaction to seeing Andrew Steel. I felt that we were there on sufferance; the officials in the court would prefer to get on with their business without having people present who were emotionally involved.

The key officials were introduced. The Honourable Justice Stephen Alliott was the judge; the prosecuting counsel on behalf of the Crown Prosecution Service was Miss Ann Rafferty, and the defence counsel Mr Trott.

The centre of the court seemed to be quite separate from the surrounding areas. The people there were mainly dressed in archaic costumes. In their grey, tightly curled wigs stretching above black robes they looked like bald-headed eagles, hovering over papers tied in dull-pink ribbons. In the jury box and the public gallery, people were dressed in everyday clothes.

Ruth's ex-partner, Tom, was the first witness for the prosecution. This was the first time we had seen him since the funeral. His face was pale beneath his fair wavy hair. He looked unfamiliar dressed in a suit; we had always seen in him casual clothes.

He was asked to describe his relationship with Andrew Steel. They had been friends for some years, but had drifted apart and then met up again.

On the evening of the Thursday, 1 February, Tom had been at the flat of his new partner, Claire. Andrew Steel was also there, along with a young woman called Libby. Tom said that Andrew Steel had been a regular user of LSD, taking it about once a week, and had brought some with him to the flat. Tom, Claire and Andrew Steel all took some LSD. During the evening, there had been a murder drama on the television called *I The Jury*, but the sound was turned down and none of them were watching it closely.

Andrew Steel had his own flat, but spent very little time there because he didn't like being on his own. Tom said he had never known Andrew Steel to be violent after taking LSD.

It was after midnight, and already Friday, 2 February, when Andrew Steel said that he wanted some more drugs and would go to a supplier he knew in Finsbury Park to get them. He returned early in the morning and 'seemed depressed', but Tom put this down to the fact that he was going to attend his grandfather's funeral and was finding it hard to get ready to go. Tom urged him to go to the funeral, saying that he should be there.

Mr Trott, the defence counsel, had no questions, so Tom was dismissed from the witness stand.

Libby was then called to give evidence. She said that she had been in a relationship with Andrew Steel for some months and he had not been violent in his relationship with her. He had shown her a flick knife on one occasion and said he had carried it for about a week for self-protection. Again, there were no questions from Mr Trott.

Miss Rafferty, the prosecution counsel, distributed to the jury a map showing the locations of Claire's flat, Ruth's house, and the route of the night-bus service that runs through North London to Enfield. She emphasised that Andrew Steel had undertaken a complex series of journeys in the early hours of Friday morning, from Palmers Green to Finsbury Park, from Finsbury Park to Enfield and then back to Palmers Green, all on public transport.

This completed the first day of the trial. We returned home and telephoned members of the family and others who had asked to be kept informed of what was happening.

Second day of the trial, Tuesday 22 January 1991

A court official read out the statement from the manager of the wine merchants where Tom used to work. Andrew Steel and Tom had gone there together on the Friday morning to pick up the wages owed to Tom. The manager had seen Andrew Steel before; she said he 'was usually on drugs' but had always been pleasant to her. On that morning, he was agitated and wanted to get away; he used the toilet at the premises several times while they were there.

Evidence was read out from the statement made by the doctor at a local hospital who had seen Andrew Steel on Friday evening at the police station about an injury to his thumb. It was bruised, not broken, and a support was fitted. The doctor found him to be emotional, weeping and complaining of a headache and asthma symptoms; he also said that he had been affected by taking LSD and cannabis, and that his thumb had been hit by a cooking pot. I remembered Matt, the detective sergeant, had told me that Ruth had tried to defend herself with a saucepan when Andrew Steel first attacked her in the kitchen. He was given paracetamol and something to relieve his asthma by the doctor, and judged fit to be interviewed. In the middle of the night, he was taken to the hospital where his thumb was plastered and body-fluid samples were taken from him.

Excerpts from the statements made by Sheila (Ruth's work colleague and friend) and James (Ruth's new partner) were also read out, recounting their visit to the house to find out why Ruth had not come to work. They had seen two men outside the house. Tom was trying to calm Andrew Steel, who was screaming and running around. Tom told them that Ruth was dead in her bedroom.

The first witness to give evidence on the second day was Ruth's elderly neighbour, the one who had written to tell me that she had heard Ruth's screams. She looked very frail, and we could see her trembling even though she was at the front of the large court and we were at the back, a considerable distance away from her.

She said she had woken in the night, as she often did, and had gone downstairs for a drink of water, then returned to bed. She was woken by the sound of someone running up and down the adjoining stairs. She heard screams and got up and stood on her landing, feeling frightened. Then she heard water running and the bathroom light being switched on and off. The front door was slammed shut with considerable force and she heard a man's voice shouting what she realised later was likely to have been 'Ruth, Ruth'. She went back to bed, thinking that there had been either a quarrel or problems with the water that had been resolved. She wasn't certain what time she had woken up or when the door had slammed shut.

Matt Miller was called to the witness stand. He had arrived at the house at about 2.15 p.m. on 2 February with a detective constable. Matt took the first witness statement from Andrew Steel at the police station. Tom was also taken to the police station and Matt took a statement from him. At this stage, neither was under arrest.

Matt's evidence revealed that Andrew Steel was born in 1967, the year after Ruth. He had a son, who was now four years old, with a common-law wife, but had lost contact with them. Since then he had had no lasting relationship. He had been a friend of Tom's for three years.

Matt and Inspector van Thal conducted an interview with Andrew Steel on the Friday evening about the discrepancies between his and Tom's statements, particularly about the timings of his journeys in the night. Andrew Steel's clothes had been taken for forensic tests. During the interview he had said, 'I did it because Ruth had hurt Tom, I did it for him.' He also claimed that Ruth had sworn at him. Later in the interview, he cried and said, 'Why did I do it, why, why, why?'

A duty solicitor arrived at the station very late on Friday evening and it was agreed that it was too late for any further interviewing; a meeting was arranged for Saturday morning.

Matt said that Geoff Parratt, the detective superintendent, started that meeting by checking the notes of the interview held on Friday evening. Andrew Steel added details of visiting the drug dealer in Finsbury Park and said, 'Somehow I just finished up at Ruth's house,' and again suggested that he had killed Ruth for Tom. Then lunch was brought and Andrew Steel had a talk in private with the solicitor.

When the meeting was resumed, more information was revealed. Andrew Steel said he had rung the bell at the house, and as there was no answer, he had gone around the back and let himself in. Ruth had come downstairs with something wrapped around her and, standing by the kitchen door, asked why he had come to the house. She was not pleased to see him. She asked, 'Where's Tom?' and, 'What are you doing here?'

Ruth had never seen him or Tom when they had taken LSD; they had agreed that she shouldn't know of it. He had shouted at her and then didn't remember any more.

Andrew Steel had been away from Claire's flat for over two hours. When he returned, there was blood on his clothing – on the bottom of his dungarees and splashes on his top. He had a bath and decided he would not go to his grandfather's funeral.

Andrew Steel said that when they returned to the house on Friday morning after picking up Tom's wages, they saw Ruth's car and realised that she was not at work. Tom had bought some records on the way to the house that he didn't want Ruth to see, so he hid them. He owed Ruth a lot of money; she would have been furious to learn that he had spent his wages on luxuries.

Andrew Steel went up the stairs; one of Ruth's cats jumped out at him and he was frightened. Geoff Parratt said, 'You knew the body was there, didn't you?' Andrew Steel replied, 'I never meant to kill her, she was too good for that, I just freaked out, acid not an excuse; she was a nice girl. She made me tea and talked to me lots of times. I would never had killed her but for the acid.'

This completed the interview and Andrew Steel signed the statement. While this interview was taking place, two detective constables had been to the house and removed items for evidence: floor covering from the bathroom, sheet, towel, dressing gown, duvet cover, shower curtain and a towel from the bottom of the stairs. They were all blood-stained.

Early on Saturday afternoon, Andrew Steel was cautioned and a recorded statement was taken about the location of the things he had taken from the house. This statement included the following comments: 'Check the bins. I got a taxi. Don't leave me. Went to a sweet shop and got Ribena. Don't remember killing her. Why did I do it?'

Another detective constable was the next to give evidence. He had received Andrew Steel's clothing; the dungarees had cannabis in one of the pockets.

On Sunday 4 February, the detective constable had been in Andrew Steel's cell with Inspector van Thal, because Andrew Steel's mother and cousin had asked to visit him. There were papers on the cell bench, including drafts of a letter to Tom that covered several pieces of paper. Andrew Steel gestured towards a drawing, saying, 'That's where the knife is.' When Inspector van Thal picked the papers up, Andrew Steel tried to snatch them from him. These papers were produced as evidence. They were all drafts of letters to Tom, apart from one that was addressed to 'Tom and all my friends'. They all pleaded with Tom to come to see him and not to desert him. He would 'get out in five years', he said; he also cautioned 'do not have acid'. The map identified the location of Ruth's possessions that he took from the house. On the back of the map was a message to a cousin: 'Look at the back and go to it.'

'Will you come and see me when I am inside?' he asked Tom. 'It was not me that killed her, I know that my friends' he wrote in the letter to 'Tom and all my friends'.

Within an hour, the police had searched the map location and found a plastic bag containing a knife. Other items were in the same area – a wallet, credit and banking cards, cheque book, cigarettes, flannel and a neck tie.

The morning's evidence was over. One of the police officers, George, came to talk to us and said that the pathologist would be giving evidence during the afternoon and we might want to consider whether we wanted to be present. Then Miss Rafferty approached us to explain that she couldn't acknowledge our presence while the court was in session, but she wanted us to know that she realised it was harrowing for us to hear the evidence.

We left the court to go to a small café around the corner for lunch. It was hard to make sense of some of the evidence. Andrew Steel had stolen some of Ruth's possessions and hidden them with what we assumed was the knife he used to stab her. He couldn't remember killing her. He had travelled back to Claire's flat after killing Ruth, rather than to his flat. He had drawn a map and asked a relative to retrieve the knife and Ruth's possessions. What was the jury making of this?

As we arrived back to take our seats in the court, there was a disturbance in the public gallery. One of our nieces was exchanging sharp words with a member of Andrew Steel's family about seating. An usher intervened and things calmed down.

The detective constable resumed his evidence. How long would we have to wait for the pathologist? That was the evidence I had waited so long to hear – would it finally satisfy me that Ruth had died quickly? If it didn't, how would I control my feelings?

Andrew Steel had sat in the police cell with his head in hands, saying, 'Why, why, why?' After half an hour his comments were recorded. He was distressed and wailing: 'I keep having flashbacks'; 'Tom shouldn't have let me out'; 'I went round the back, Ruth opened the door. She was a nice girl.' He said that he took LSD most weekends. 'Why didn't she know? She fell over and went upstairs. She was going to call the police to get me out.'

More excerpts from written police statements taken the day after Ruth died were read out: 'It's bad stuff' (about LSD); 'She was a nice girl, Ruth; she was too good for that'; 'Went to talk to the girl'; 'Just a trip'; 'Grandfather died, his mother would be cut up'; 'Ruth should have known and not wound me up'.

The pathologist's name was called, and a dark-haired young woman, standing very upright, took the oath. In her evidence, she said that one of the major wounds would have been the first to be inflicted because 'there were no defence injuries and therefore consciousness would have been lost very quickly'. If someone is being attacked from the front, they will instinctively put their arms and hands over their face. She raised her arms very quickly to demonstrate the reaction. There were no injuries on Ruth's forearms.

*

Why couldn't someone, anyone, have explained this to me months before? Fourteen words were all it took to convince me. The continuing nightmares and obsessional thinking in the daytime that Ruth could have been saved if someone had got to the house earlier, that she had been alive and in terrible pain for hours, had all been unfounded.

*

While the pathologist was giving her evidence, the jury was looking at the photographs of Ruth and at the knife that had been plunged into her so many, many times. The knife moved from hand to hand – I couldn't see it or the photos. I didn't know if Andrew Steel had a knife with him when he entered the house, or if he had picked up one in the kitchen. I didn't want to know in case it was one of a set of cooking knives that we had given Ruth when she moved into the house.

The next witness was the police doctor. He had analysed samples taken within twenty-four hours of Ruth's death from Andrew Steel and from Ruth. In Andrew Steel, there was nicotine, paracetamol, fentomine, LSD and cannabis, but no alcohol. In Ruth, no drugs, no alcohol.

The police doctor went on to describe the effects of the drugs that Andrew Steel had taken. LSD is not prescribed in modern medicine, so because it is an illicit drug there is no quality control. This means that some doses can be stronger than others can – a variation of up to ten-times normal strength is possible: these are known as 'hot spots'. He had no knowledge of LSD causing violent behaviour. The impact of taking LSD is felt most strongly about an hour after being taken. This peak is maintained for up to an hour. Then the effect slowly wears off.

Ruth's blood was on all the items that the police had taken from the house and retrieved from Andrew Steel. There was no trace of a sexual attack. Strands of Ruth's hair were found in the neck tie. The neck tie had been cut.

There was a bus ticket in Andrew Steel's jacket. 5.01 a.m. was the time printed on the ticket; the bus was due at the stop he alighted from at 5.08 a.m. It wouldn't have taken long for him to walk to Ruth's house from the bus stop.

Inspector van Thal was then called to the witness stand. He confirmed that Andrew Steel had been charged with Ruth's murder on 3 February and had made no reply to the charge. He had never served a prison sentence.

This ended the second day's evidence. On the way home we needed to get some food shopping done. I didn't want to meet anybody we knew. I needed to save all my energy for making telephone calls to family members and the other people who wanted to know what had happened during the day. I now really knew that Ruth had died quickly. This didn't mean that she had not suffered; she had died in a horrible way and experienced great fear and terror. She hadn't known that Andrew Steel or Tom took drugs and, as far I knew, had had no experience of people whose behaviour was affected by drugs. The bruising had occurred before the stab wounds, so she had experienced pain – I couldn't bear to think of her feelings as Andrew Steel approached her with the knife in his hand. She had tried to defend herself but would have stood no chance against his greater strength.

I dreaded phoning Catherine, so newly delivered of her first child, and considered carefully how much to tell her about the day's evidence. But she had said she wanted to know what was happening, so I called her first. She sounded weary and subdued, but relieved to hear about the pathologist's evidence.

Third day of the trial, Wednesday 23 January 1991
The first two days of the trial had established the facts of what had happened. The third day started with expert witnesses reporting conflicting views on the effects of taking LSD. Dr Andrew Johns, who works at St George's Hospital in Tooting, was called on behalf of the prosecution. He is an expert in the effects of LSD.

Miss Rafferty, the prosecuting counsel, asked if the events of the case fitted with taking LSD. Dr Johns replied that the organised behaviour Andrew Steel had demonstrated was not consistent with psychotic experience. 'The ferocity of the attack – it sounds as if you would have to be crazy – but this was not necessarily due to drugs. It is common for one stab to lead to more in cases where drugs are not involved. Partial amnesia is well known among people who have experienced a traumatic event who have not taken drugs. Andrew Steel took items from the house and hid them. This is organised behaviour and not consistent with LSD.'

He continued, 'LSD is not known to cause permanent damage to the brain either in structure or function.'

He was then cross-examined by the defence counsel, Mr Trott.

He quickly moved to the crux of the defence, citing Section 2 of the Homicide Act 1957, which gives 'injury' as one of the grounds for diminished responsibility. Mr Trott asked Dr Johns if LSD could 'injure' the brain, either by itself or in combination with other drugs.

'No,' said Dr Johns. 'LSD breaks down the barriers between reality and unreality, but it doesn't justify diminished responsibility. The savage wounds inflicted on the victim don't fit the symptoms seen in someone who has brain injuries.'

Mr Trott asked no further questions, but Miss Rafferty had a further point to put to the court: 'Between 3 and 5 a.m. Andrew Steel had travelled from Palmers Green to Finsbury Park, to Turnpike Lane, back to Palmers Green and then to Enfield. All this journeying had been done on public transport; surely this demonstrated that he had the capacity to think and carry out plans?' Dr Johns agreed.

The defence case didn't look convincing to us, but what were the jury thinking? They were still attentive.

The atmosphere in the court grew more tense when the only defence witness was summoned to appear. When we saw him, I realised that he was the man I had seen the day before lounging in the seating within the court. I had wondered if he was a journalist, but he wasn't taking any notes.

Professor Edwards is a forensic psychiatrist and Professor of Addictive Behaviour at London University; he also worked at the Maudsley Bethlem hospital. He had been in practice for thirty-two years. A thick-set man with a full head of greying hair, he looked quite at ease in the court and took the oath in a loud, confident voice.

He had interviewed Andrew Steel while he was on remand in Brixton Prison in December. During a two-hour session, he took a history of his health, sexual development and drug use, particularly of LSD.

He found no evidence of any mental illness, past or present, and Andrew Steel's IQ was within the normal range. The professor described him as a child who had been bullied at school to the point of truanting, which led to his referral to a child-guidance clinic. Andrew Steel was also asthmatic. He hadn't been a juvenile delinquent. On this basis, the professor concluded that there were no roots for the development of a psychopathic personality.

Professor Edwards found Andrew Steel to be 'good-natured, a follower rather than a leader and likely to apologise to someone who had trodden on his foot'. The relationship between him and Ruth was 'brotherly/sisterly'. There had been no sexual relationship, no rows, no grudges between them. Andrew Steel had described Ruth as a 'normal, likeable young woman'.

The professor had listened to Andrew Steel's account of the night Ruth died and had considered the role that LSD might have played. Andrew Steel was a regular user of LSD and took up to one-and-a-half tablets at a time. The events of the night were congruent with a large dose and severe reaction. The effects of LSD can last up to twenty-four hours. The statements given and signed by the defendant demonstrated the effects of amnesia – 'It all fits with a large dose'. However, Professor Edwards could not rule out that the statements could also be consistent with the behaviour of someone who was not on drugs.

'Ruth had wound him up rather than talked him down,' he said, and this had caused temporary insanity. This was the first time that Ruth had been mentioned in any way other than as the victim of a brutal murder. Was this the only ploy that the defence could use, to say that if Ruth had reacted differently, she might not have been attacked? Were they suggesting that her death was her fault? How would Professor Edwards have reacted, I wondered, if someone had come into his home in the early hours of the morning and behaved in such a manner?

The night journeying and the 'patchy remembering' were 'odd', and he couldn't explain this. The judge asked if hiding the weapon was a rational act. Professor Edwards' conclusion was that the story fitted with LSD intoxication, which he described as a 'chemical concussion'. Mr Trott summarised by asking if this evidence meant that the defendant was suffering from a substantial mental impairment. The reply was a terse 'Yes', supplemented by, 'On the balance of probability, Andrew Steel was suffering from abnormality of mind and was substantially impaired at the time of the attack.' Professor Edwards accepted that he had only heard Andrew Steel's interpretation of the events and admitted that he thought it was odd that he had taken things from the house and hidden them, then drawn a map of their location.

This evidence raised several questions for me. The interview had taken place ten months after Ruth's death; therefore the original defence counsel could not have been prepared for a trial in October. Andrew Steel had had plenty of time to reflect on what had happened and perhaps to put forward an account that would not be the whole truth. This evidence on the effects of LSD was markedly different to that given by Dr Johns and seemed a weak basis for the defence. I had no knowledge, either directly or indirectly, of the effects of LSD. I had read a short book about it but had never, to my knowledge, seen anyone who had taken it while they were intoxicated. What would the jury make of these different accounts? I still had no sense of how the evidence was building – was it towards a conviction of murder or of manslaughter?

Professor Edwards was the only defence witness. As Andrew Steel would not be put on the witness stand, we would have no opportunity to hear his own account of events or to hear him cross-examined by the prosecution.

The court rose for the lunch recess, and we emerged into the dismal February day to walk around the corner to the small café. The noise of the traffic and crowds of people were a marked contrast to the quiet, measured manner of the court. How quickly we had got into a routine. It was a relief to walk about; neither of us was used to sitting still for long periods. In the court, we were conscious that any movement on our part might be misinterpreted and lead to our being evicted.

The consultant forensic psychiatrist witness, Dr Bowden, was the first witness in the afternoon and the last to be called. He had been present throughout the trial, had read all the trial documents and had undertaken two assessments of Andrew Steel. Dr Bowden had first seen him at Brixton Prison on the Tuesday, 6 February. The interview was written up in November, over nine months later, and covered one-and-a-half pages of text. During the interview, Andrew Steel had been tense, agitated, asthmatic and had talked about drugs.

Dr Bowden agreed with Professor Edwards about the effects

of LSD and said, 'It might have been helpful to have seen Andrew Steel soon after he was charged, but this was not significant in my view.'

Miss Rafferty asked how he explained the 'seemingly motiveless behaviour' – no explanations or motives had been established.

The only, or the major, issue was intoxication, in Dr Bowden's view. Was Andrew Steel legally insane, or was he so intoxicated by LSD that he could not form intent? The evidence did not indicate insanity: there was plenty to indicate that he could act rationally and that his behaviour was governed by reason; for example, the journey between several locations before arriving in Enfield. He thought that intoxication was implausible as a cause of injury.

Each year an average of 700 murder charges are made; it is therefore a rare behaviour. It is not uncommon for injuries to be inflicted after death, but Dr Bowden agreed that there are very few murders with this number of injuries. Once someone has inflicted serious wounds, it is common for them not to stop until their victim is dead. Forty per cent of people who kill have amnesia, irrespective of whether they have taken drugs.

At the end of this evidence, the jury were dismissed so that the judge could go over case law with the defence and prosecution counsels. He indicated that the prosecution would have to establish Andrew Steel's intent to kill for a murder verdict. The defence would have to demonstrate that he had insufficient capacity to form intent to kill for a manslaughter verdict. The plea of diminished responsibility hinged on definition and whether the jury agreed that he should be found guilty of the lesser charge.

This ended the third day of the trial. Again we travelled home through the rush hour, trains crowded with commuters, and arrived home in the dark.

As I made the round of evening phone calls, people were asking what verdict we thought would be returned. I couldn't say; I didn't know. I didn't want to be disappointed if a manslaughter verdict was returned. I did want the police to be rewarded for their work and Andrew Steel to be punished for what he had done, but there would be no pleasure in a verdict of guilty of murder.

I ate comfort food, chocolate, cheese, stodgy, fatty things, unable to settle to do anything in what was left of the evening after the calls were finished. Would the jury be sent out to consider their verdict the next day? I had a long bath, hoping this would relax me, but no sleep came that night. I lay in bed for a long time before giving up – it was 2 a.m. I went downstairs and listened to the tape of the requiem by John Rutter. I needed to get a grip on my feelings so as not to lose control in public. As ever, my fear was that if I started to cry in public, I would not be able to stop. Gradually and very slowly, the night passed until it was time to start the day.

Fourth day of the trial, Thursday 24 January 1991
Each time I entered the court and sat down, I tried to detach myself in an emotional sense from what was going on, and to concentrate objectively on the facts being put before the jury. While I know that law is important, I do find its detail boring. It occurred to me that perhaps the 'experts' and legal people were quite excited at the prospect of this case creating some legal precedent if the defence were able to prove that Andrew Steel's brain had been 'injured' by taking LSD.

The jury were not present during the morning. This was a long session detailing many past cases and detailed aspects of the law. It was hard to concentrate.

Mr Trott presented the case law that would support his plea for a manslaughter verdict. He quoted many cases, nearly all of them from more than twenty years earlier. None of them included drugs: they were all alcohol-related.

The judge said, 'The defendant cannot shelter behind voluntary intake of LSD.' He went on, 'In the thirty-three years since the Homicide Act 1957 was passed, "injury" has only been used once as a defence and was not successful. The defence expert witness, Professor Edwards, has presented "a novel aspect in this case" by introducing the position of *this* dose on *this* occasion'.

Miss Rafferty said, 'There is no case law to support the defence.' Diminished responsibility has to be established by the defence. This could only be done if the jury accepted that the defendant had an abnormality of mind that had been caused through 'injury', or that his behaviour in response to taking LSD had been markedly different from his previous experience of the drug. Professor Edwards (the only defence witness) had had only one interview with Andrew Steel and had accepted his interpretation of the events. 'Injury' had been used in a medical rather than a legal sense by the professor.

When the jury returned, the judge reminded them that there could be no acquittal because Andrew Steel had admitted that he killed Ruth.

He explained that they would hear summing-up statements from the prosecution and the defence counsel. While they were listening, they should be considering whether the prosecution had proved it was murder: did Andrew Steel intend to kill, what was the impact of intoxication and was the plea of diminished responsibility reasonable? Had the defence proved abnormality of mind — they should disregard the influence of drugs. The evidence from the expert witnesses had conflicted: did they accept that of Professor Edwards, who had said that LSD had injured Andrew Steel's brain, or the views of Dr Johns and Dr Bowden, who denied that LSD could injure someone's brain?

The judge said that he would be seeking a unanimous verdict, but would direct on a majority verdict if necessary.

Miss Rafferty summed up the prosecution case, emphasising all the evidence that showed Andrew Steel thinking about his actions: he had travelled at night, using public transport to make several journeys; he had stolen items from the house before leaving and then hidden them; he had made a map to show their location.

Mr Trott could only offer in defence that the impact of the dose of LSD had injured Andrew Steel's brain and caused his violent behaviour just for the time it took for him to attack Ruth and kill her.

The afternoon wore on. Our hopes of the jury being sent out to come back with a verdict that day were vanishing. I wanted the trial to be over and done with. Much of the day had been taken up with crawling over cases that seemed to me to have no bearing on the facts presented by the defence.

The judge started his direction of the jury. He summarised the key points of the evidence and pointed out that they should not be influenced by the fact that Andrew Steel had not given evidence — he was entitled to remain silent. He described Ruth's injuries in some detail — so little of her body was untouched. He commented that there were still unresolved aspects — how did Andrew Steel get into the house, and what was the significance of the tie with Ruth's hair in it?

It was now late afternoon. The judge adjourned the hearing, saying that he would give his final directions to the jury in the morning.

The day hadn't brought the conclusion of the trial. We

couldn't even be certain that the trial wouldn't go on into a second week if the jury needed more than a day to consider their verdict.

The round of phone calls circled around the same themes: what would Andrew Steel be convicted of, and what sentence would he be given? I was exhausted and retreated to the bath for a long soak and to read something totally unconnected with the week's events.

Fifth day of the trial, Friday 25 January 1991

I slept better that night, but was still very on edge the next morning. We left the house for what we hoped would be our final visit to the Old Bailey.

Everyone was in place in the court. We now knew where to look and what functions were carried out at each location. Everyone rose as the judge entered, and Andrew Steel was called up from the cells. Yet again, we looked at the back of his head. We knew little more about him after hearing all the evidence and still had no understanding of his actions. He had sat quietly throughout the trial, hardly moving.

The final directions to the jury were concise. Their task was to decide whether Andrew Steel had committed murder or manslaughter. It would be murder if they felt he had the capacity to form intent to kill or to harm Ruth; manslaughter if they accepted that he had suffered from an abnormality of mind due to an injury to his brain. A unanimous verdict was asked for, but further direction would be given if this could not be achieved.

The jury filed out through the door at the side of the jury benches at 10.15.

Two police officers, George and Tracy, came towards us and said that we could go with them to the canteen on an upper floor to wait for the verdict. We sat with teas and coffees at a plain table.

We talked about the trial and speculated about the outcome. I expressed my disappointment that we had learned little more about Andrew Steel and why he had killed Ruth. George told us that his flat was full of stolen property: he stole to pay for drugs. We also heard that Andrew Steel had a history of violence towards women, though he had never been charged with any offence. He had broken the arm of one woman, and the police had asked two others to give evidence at the trial, but they had been too afraid. He wasn't the meek and mild person portrayed by the defence; he had a history of attacking women.

The time dragged by. It got to lunchtime and we had some sandwiches and chocolate biscuits. Geoff Parratt came to talk to us; he clearly expected a murder verdict. The police wanted Andrew Steel put away and did little to conceal their contempt for him.

The low ceilings of the room pushed down; my head was pounding. The afternoon wore on and still we sat, losing count of the cups of tea we had drunk.

Finally, at 2.45 p.m., we were called to return to the court. All the court officials took their places; the jury filed in and took their seats. We all stood up as the judge entered and Andrew Steel was called to take his place in the dock.

There was a strange sensation of being on a film set as the words 'Members of the jury, have you reached a verdict?' were uttered. How many times had I heard these words before, having no special interest in the response. The foreman replied, 'Yes.' And was the verdict unanimous? 'Yes.' And what was the verdict? 'Guilty of murder.' I glanced up at Andrew Steel, but only saw his hunched shoulders.

Mr Trott was invited to make a statement to say why Andrew Steel should receive a lesser rather than a greater sentence.

He had three points to offer:

—Andrew Steel had said he would never take drugs again.

—He had showed remorse: 'I did it for Tom'; 'Ruth was a nice girl.'

—He was a young man.

I felt strongly that these were insubstantial excuses rather than reasons. Andrew Steel shouldn't have taken drugs in the first place. Saying that he had killed Ruth for someone else and that she was a nice girl didn't demonstrate remorse: they were an excuse and an opinion, and he was old enough to know that harming other people is wrong.

All eyes were now on the judge. He asked Andrew Steel to stand up and addressed him directly: 'The only sentence I can pass is a mandatory life sentence. I will make a recommendation of the time you will serve to the Home Secretary.'

Before Andrew Steel was taken down to the cells for the last time, he looked up at the public gallery and gave a slight wave.

The judge then turned to the jury and thanked them for their service before dismissing them. He told them that he realised it had been a harrowing case for them to hear and that there were still many unanswered questions. Then, much to my surprise, he said, 'I want you to know that I fully agree with your verdict.' Until that moment, we had no idea of his personal opinion about the case. I don't know how unusual it is for a judge to say such a thing, but it helped us to know that this experienced judge felt the right decision had been reached.

We sat for a while after the court had emptied, then George and Tracy came back into the court and we walked with them to the corridor outside. Until then I had managed to stay calm, but Tracy's gentle hand on my shoulder released the taut control. I clutched at her. 'Don't cry now,' she said.

*

It was hard to know how to feel about the verdict. I knew that the number of years served as a life sentence could vary considerably. I had always felt that it was wrong for the term to be decided by a politician, rather than by the judge in the trial. In murder, as in other crimes, there are degrees of severity. The verdict also left a great gap: we didn't know when or even if we would be advised of the tariff (as the length of the sentence is known), or what the longer-term implications would be for Andrew Steel. Presumably, this would mean that he, too, would endure a delay before his fate was known.

We went back up to the canteen, drank more tea, and tried to rejoice with the police officers, who were jubilant at the success of their efforts to bring Andrew Steel to justice. Geoff Parratt had been worried that the result might be a manslaughter verdict with a low-tariff sentence.

It was the rush hour as we travelled home, drained and yet relieved that this milestone was behind us. How I longed to walk in and find a meal magically on the table. Maybe it was better to have to think about everyday things – get the ingredients out, prepare the food, cook it, set the table, eat and clear away – before the fifth evening of making phone calls.

Most people were astonished that we didn't know how many years the sentence would be or to which prison Andrew Steel would be sent. The reactions to the verdict varied. Someone said that they wished that capital punishment were still in force, and if it were, he would go and offer to swing on Andrew Steel's legs. Another felt that Andrew Steel must have had a raw deal from life to act so viciously.

The trial had been a huge disappointment, leaving so many questions unanswered. The only person who could answer them was Andrew Steel, and he hadn't given evidence, hadn't been cross-examined. I felt cheated of hearing an account directly from him. I was left still trying to understand why Andrew Steel had killed Ruth.

When I phoned one of our nieces, who had been in court throughout the trial, she said sadly, 'I needed to see that he was sorry, and he wasn't.' She was shaken by the verdict of murder: 'It means that he meant to kill Ruth; it wasn't an accident.'

Chapter Nine
The aftermath of the trial

MORE PHONE CALLS had to be made over the weekend to inform family and friends about the outcome of the trial. One call was to Jane, a member of the executive committee of SANDS, the bereavement charity I had worked for. She had helped me to contact the pathologist when I was trying to get a copy of the post-mortem report. Jane was a probation officer working on the lifers' unit at Wormwood Scrubs, where life-sentence prisoners from the London area are transferred after sentence. On hearing the verdict, she said that Andrew Steel would be transferred to Wormwood Scrubs, because all life-sentence prisoners convicted in the London area go there. She said it wouldn't be possible for him to remain at the Scrubs because of the connection between her and our family, and she would have to go and talk to the governor.

A few days later, the phone rang. It was Jane. She told me that a colleague had been to see Andrew Steel to tell him that he would have to be transferred to another prison to serve his sentence and the reason for this. The colleague had said that Andrew Steel 'went bright white' when he was told. Jane didn't realise that this was a very startling statement, as Andrew Steel is black. He had asked to meet Jane and she wanted to know if we would have any objections. I said I would call her back after I had discussed it with Vic. He had no objections, and I thought this would be a good opportunity to find out more about Andrew Steel and to ask for answers to some questions which hadn't been resolved by the evidence given at the trial. I also decided to send a message to him. I asked

Jane to tell him that I hoped he would accept any assistance offered to him to help him to understand why he had done what he had done. I wanted him to use any opportunities he was offered to extend his skills and education and to resolve to use the rest of his life in positive ways both for himself and for others. I wanted, but couldn't bring myself, to send him a message of forgiveness.

At 6.30 p.m. on Thursday 31 January, the phone rang. It was Jane. She had seen Andrew Steel for about three-quarters of an hour earlier that day, and she had quite a lot to tell me.

I pulled a pad of paper towards me and picked up a pen:

—*terribly, terribly sorry*
—*how much he respected Ruth*
—*grateful for the message*
—*knows nothing about the necklace*
—*back door was open and he walked in — had done it before and Ruth sorted him out*
—*2nd post-mortem — he didn't know about it*
—*never heard the full extent of injuries until the court*
—*asked lawyers before the trial if he could make a cross for Ruth and they said no*
—*disorientated*
—*he was aware that we were there in the Old Bailey but couldn't bear to look at us*
—*how are they managing?*
—*very upset but didn't avoid things*
—*family not seen him*
—*he will tell his family of Jane's visit if they come*
—*he would be at the prison for about a month before being transferred*

Jane said she had told him he could make a cross, but it wouldn't mean that we would be willing to accept it. She hadn't concealed the terrible suffering he had caused. Her impression was that he did show remorse for killing Ruth, but that his major preoccupation was self-pity for his own situation.

I sat upstairs for half an hour after putting the phone down. What had this information revealed? Taking the bitterest view, it showed one outcome of Ruth being a caring person – if she hadn't helped him, she might still be alive.

Did I want to think any more about Andrew Steel? Could I afford the emotional energy – what would be the point? Jane had said that he wasn't my responsibility but that of the prison service, and that was true. However, I found it impossible to stop thinking about him. I knew how I felt about what he had done: I hated it. Given his previous history of injuring women, the murder verdict had to be the right one. He should be removed from society until he had learned to control his violent urges and understood what lay behind them.

Yet this conversation had revealed more about him, made him more of a human being than a tabloid 'monster'. He was self-pitying: that was good – it would have been worse if he had shown no emotion. He hadn't asked for the second post-mortem, hadn't even been aware of it, so it wasn't his fault that we had to wait for weeks to hold Ruth's funeral.

I told Vic what Jane had said. He made no response.

The next day, Friday 1 February, I was on edge as we ate our evening meal. It had been the Friday evening, the year before, when the doorbell rang and within a few minutes our lives had been thrown into turmoil. I had been to see Catherine during the morning and we had talked about Ruth and what she might be doing if she were still alive. I had bought a pack of blue tapered candles and planned to burn one on the first anniversary of Ruth's death. I would put it in a turned-wood candleholder made on the day of her funeral by a friend. On my return home, my neighbour came out of his front door and said, 'I've taken something in for you.' It was a bouquet of blue and white flowers. Matt Miller, the detective sergeant who had been so supportive to us, had enclosed a card with the flowers. He must have made a special trip to come to our house, and I was very sorry that I had missed seeing him.

Very early on Saturday morning, I woke and looked at the clock, and realised that it was around the time that Andrew Steel had left Claire's flat. I couldn't get back to sleep, so I went downstairs and watched the time clicking by on the video's digital clock. 'At this time, he was travelling to Finsbury Park.' 'By this time he had arrived at the house.' 'This is when he left the house.' I played the training video, without the sound on, watching Ruth, so animated and involved in her work.

The day passed quietly, Vic and I companionable but pursuing separate activities. I lit the blue candle and, comforted by its gentle glow, wrote letters to the many people who had sent letters, cards and flowers during the period of the trial and for the anniversary of Ruth's death.

Now we had passed all the major landmarks: the first Christmas, the trial, the first anniversary. I was crying less, but still finding it difficult to be cheerful. I knew it wasn't good to keep such a tight rein on my feelings, but it was unnerving to find that situations I usually found funny still triggered tears rather than laughter. Music, which had always been a great pleasure, was now another source of pain.

We planned a holiday for May to give ourselves something to look forward to. We would go to the Isles of Scilly, where we had had shared so many happy family experiences. On this trip we would be able to see Ruth's seat, which was already on St Martin's.

A few weeks after the trial, we had a phone call from a

police officer we had had no previous contact with, saying that she would like to come to see us to return the items that had been held by the police for the trial.

She was a pleasant, brisk young woman. She held out a black plastic rubbish sack. Inside was a clear plastic folder. In the folder were Ruth's credit card, cheque book, Filofax, two packets of cigarettes and other small items. There was no sign of her necklace. Vic signed the form acknowledging receipt. I was calm while the police officer was with us, but after she left I vented my feelings of disgust. How could they do this? It was a horrible thing to do. These were Ruth's possessions that Andrew Steel had touched — he had stolen them, hidden them together with the knife that he killed her with. They had been returned to us as garbage.

*

The Lord Chancellor had responded to my letter about seating in court. I had written to him again since the trial to raise a number of issues: the repercussions of giving a witness statement, second post-mortems, and asking for information about the length of the sentence Andrew Steel had been given. His Department had sent sections of my letter to the appropriate government departments.

The first Department to respond was on the third issue: the Lifers' Unit at the Home Office, saying that enquiries were being made. In May, I received an extraordinary letter that told me it wasn't possible for the information to be given to me, as it was confidential. However, the letter then went on to give me a series of clues. I phoned, asked to speak to the civil servant and said, 'If I say a number, will you say yes or no?' I said thirteen and she said, 'Yes.'

This meant that Andrew Steel would be in prison until

2003, and even then he would not be released unless the prison were confident that he would harm no one else in future. On release, he would be subject to stringent conditions. He would have to maintain close links with the probation service; if his behaviour gave any cause for concern, he could be put back in prison. He would still be young enough to establish a new life for himself; he would be in his mid-thirties when he left prison after completing his sentence.

Was thirteen years 'enough'? Was any length of time 'enough'? Because the sentencing procedure is so secretive, it wasn't possible to get a clear idea of what was 'usual'. I felt under no personal threat from Andrew Steel or his family, and by the time he was released our lives would be very different. It was quite likely that we would have retired and perhaps moved.

What troubled me was that he could just 'sit it out' in prison. He would be with people who knew neither him nor us, and I couldn't see how he could be helped to understand what he had done and why he had done it. Jane had said that he was sorry, but I hadn't heard this directly. Other people had said that I should forget him, but this was impossible.

Still brooding, I prepared to go on holiday to the Isles of Scilly. The day after we arrived, we went to the harbour and got on the launch to St Martin's. As it moored, I glanced up towards the cottages on Signal Row. The place where Ruth's seat would be was obscured by the turn in the road below the cottages. I hung back, wanting the rest of the people to disappear before we started to walk up the hill. Suddenly, dreadful, harsh sobs arose from my chest. I couldn't stop them. I turned away and pretended to be looking at the profusion of wild flowers on the high stone walls. Tears streamed down. I couldn't stop them. I sat down on the path. Vic stood nearby, looking embarrassed. After a few minutes, I got up and said that I had collected myself. As we turned the corner, I could see the seat.

The strong, simple, wooden seat had been made entirely on the islands, and the woodcarver had inscribed 'GIVEN IN LOVING MEMORY OF RUTH MORELAND' along the top rail. Around its legs wild flowers twined; bits of weathered blue polypropylene rope and orange floats were nearby in the grass. Sitting on the seat, we could see the turn to the beach we regarded as 'our place', the panoramic view of the wide silver sweep of the bay and the single made-up road disappearing towards Middle Town. I got my camera out and took photos. We were very pleased with this memorial to Ruth and hoped that many people would find it a good place to take a rest.

Filled with sunshine and the good air of St Martin's, we travelled back on the launch to our self-catering flat. The rest of the week passed quietly, with lots of walking, reading and knitting.

On our return home, I started to work on a presentation for a training session for Victim Support. They had asked me to contribute to a session for volunteers who would help families after a murder.

I wanted to demonstrate the complexity of the impact of murder and show that Victim Support volunteers would be faced with a variety of reactions and needs among the individual members of families of murder victims.

I asked a number of people – Catherine, my mother, James, and some friends – to write something about their reactions to Ruth's death and what they had observed about the impact on our family. These accounts would be helpful in preparing for the talk. When they arrived, they provided far more than I expected.

I hadn't fully appreciated the severity and the longevity of the impact on the people who were at more of a distance. One friend whose children were young expressed the dreadful fear that had been forced on her – were her daughters' futures safe? Another friend was astounded that something like this could have happened in our circle. Most of us had led quite conventional lives, married for many years, living in suburbia, working hard. Her daughter had just left home to live alone in a flat in a town some miles away. My friend's confidence was shaken considerably as to the advisability of young women living away from their parental home.

James's outpourings of rage and anguish had helped me soon after Ruth's death. He was still angry, very angry.

The pack of papers everyone was given as they arrived for the Victim Support training session included a sheet setting out the figures for homicides in the London boroughs for 1990. In Enfield, there were six; one of those six was Ruth.

I had already received a draft programme for the day, so I knew that another parent would also be speaking, and that our session was the first of the day. I was introduced to Mrs Fuller whose son, Clifford, had been killed in 1986. She would speak first. She had spoken before about her experiences for Victim Support.

The audience took their places. Mrs Fuller and I were escorted to the stage. The opening formalities over, she stood up and started her presentation. Her son's killer had been found guilty of manslaughter. Clifford had been walking in the street when someone he had never met attacked him. The family endured a delay of months before they could hold his funeral, and every day Mrs Fuller had to walk past the mortuary where his body was held during the long wait. A manslaughter verdict meant that the sentence was short, and the killer had already been released from prison.

I wondered how she had endured walking past the mortuary. At least for us Hornsey was too far away for that to have happened. The man who killed her son lived locally; she might pass him in the street. This wasn't likely to happen to us.

Then it was my turn. I had tried to consider the needs of the audience of about sixty people, which included police officers, Victim Support scheme co-ordinators, volunteers and committee members.

From my work at SANDS, I was aware of some of the difficulties the volunteers would face. Following a tragic event, they are with people they have never met, and they can't 'make it better'. The balance between practical and emotional support is hard to maintain. The length of time that families would need help would vary considerably and some would reject offers of help – as we ourselves had done.

I outlined our experiences following Ruth's death, and stressed the frustration I had felt at information being withheld from us. I resented not having access to information that other people, whose lives were not directly affected, could obtain because of their occupation. It had taken considerable effort, which had drained my already depleted energies, both to see Ruth at the mortuary and to find out the details about her injuries.

The coffee break followed, and a police officer approached me. He thanked me for speaking and said that he had learned a hard lesson. He had worked as the senior officer on a number of murder cases and had always tried to protect the families, as he saw it. He had done this by withholding information that he thought might be upsetting for them.

Some volunteers from local Victim Support schemes had

been surprised to hear that we had not taken up the offer made by the police to be put in touch with our local scheme on the day Ruth died. I explained that our immediate need was to be in touch with our family and friends. Also, my reactions and Vic's were different: he did not want 'outsiders' to be involved any more than was absolutely essential. Although I didn't say so, I also knew that I was uncomfortable with the reversal of my former professional situation. I had been accustomed to being someone who people contacted for help, not being the one asking for and accepting help.

Another police officer said that it was brave of me to talk about Ruth's death. Was it brave? It was, after all, a protected environment, for people who were wanting to help others who had suffered in the aftermath of murder. It was an opportunity for me to be able to talk about Ruth, and it had enabled me to put the events following her death into some kind of order in my mind.

*

Another opportunity to talk about Ruth soon presented itself: Jane asked if I would go the prison where she worked and talk to her colleagues in the probation service.

Early in July, seventeen months after Ruth's death, I travelled to the prison, walking from the nearest Underground station in warm sunshine. The reception desk had my details and I was quickly let in through the metal and stone entrance. Jane was waiting on the other side to meet me, we went across a wide yard to one of the buildings. Up lots of stairs, down long corridors, we entered a bright room with several people already there, eating their lunch.

When everyone had arrived, Jane introduced me and explained how we had come to know each other through SANDS and the role she had played as intermediary after

Andrew Steel had been transferred to the prison after the trial.

Jane had asked me to 'tell the story' so that her colleagues could hear about the impact of a murder on the family of the victim. In the discussion that followed, a few of the probation officers mentioned that some offenders had wanted to contact the victims of their crime. It was evident that there was a variety of views about contact between offenders and the victims' families.

One probation officer maintained that her role was to support offenders, and therefore it was inappropriate to do anything that might harm her clients. Very few of them had any experience of contact between victims and offenders, and those that did spoke of exchanges of letters rather than any direct contact. Some had positively encouraged lifers to contact their victims, but this seemed to be more for the lifers' benefit than for the victims. Others had blocked any contact. One lifer had asked one of the probation officers to send a letter from him to the victim's family. She had refused. What stood out for me was that it seemed that none of them had considered the need to inform the victims about a request from a lifer, to see if contact would be welcomed or not, or indeed to facilitate contact if this were requested by a victim.

I hadn't really thought about the role of the probation service before, but I came away feeling pensive about the power that the officers held and how protective they were of their clients.

★

Following my experience of giving these talks, I began to feel more and more that I wanted to meet, or at least make contact with, Andrew Steel. I needed to understand why he had killed Ruth; he was the only person who could tell me. There were several possible routes, but I had to accept that he might not be willing to be in touch with me. Victim Support had suggested it would be helpful if I wrote something about my experience for their volunteers, and I would be meeting with some of their staff to discuss ideas soon after going to Wormwood Scrubs. I decided to use this meeting to explore alternative ways of making contact with Andrew Steel and to ask if they could help me.

Martin Wright, the Victim Support policy officer, had a long-standing involvement with mediation, and was one of the staff members present. I already knew that I could write to Andrew Steel to ask for a visitor's order, but didn't feel that this was the best approach. If he refused, or didn't respond, it might close the door forever. I felt that an approach through an intermediary might be received as being less threatening and therefore might have a better chance of succeeding. Martin had heard of no one else who had tried to do what I was attempting, but offered to explore possible routes on my behalf.

Martin contacted the chaplain at Wakefield Prison, where I had been told Andrew Steel had been sent from Wormwood Scrubs. When Martin phoned to report back, he said, 'Andrew Steel isn't at Wakefield Prison and they have no record of him.' This was a surprise, but Martin said he would be able to find out which prison Andrew Steel was in. He found out that Andrew Steel had been sent to Gartree Prison. The chaplain there agreed to talk to the staff who worked most closely with him about my request.

The weeks ticked by, and Martin heard nothing further from the chaplain. One afternoon I was feeling very fed up about the long delay in hearing anything about my request. I phoned the prison and asked to speak to the chaplain myself.

He was very startled to hear from me directly. I asked when I was going to hear if it would be possible to make arrangements to meet Andrew Steel. After offering condolences on Ruth's death, he became very defensive and several times said, 'Our responsibility is towards the prisoner.' Something in me snapped and I shouted at him, 'And who is going to take responsibility for me?' He didn't respond to this, but said, 'It isn't helpful that the grandmother has been in touch as well.'

This was news to me. I knew immediately that it would be my mother rather than my mother-in-law. Apparently, she had been in touch with the prison and had corresponded with Andrew Steel without mentioning it to me. I was very shaken by this information and felt that it had been a great mistake to phone on impulse. I was disappointed and upset that the chaplain seemed to have little thought for my feelings, and I wondered if Andrew Steel even knew of my request.

I phoned Martin and 'confessed'. He said he would phone the chaplain. I said that I would not want to meet Andrew Steel around the anniversary of Ruth's death, and perhaps for everyone's sake there should be some time boundary set within which the meeting should be arranged or the quest abandoned. A week later, Martin wrote:

21st October 1991

I spoke to the chaplain again. He says the probation officer wants to do 'ongoing work' with Andrew Steel, who, he says, is very remorseful, with a great weight of guilt, but is not yet in a frame of mind where he could handle a meeting. He was 'gobsmacked' when your message reached him in Wormwood Scrubs.

The chaplain fully understood your feelings about the timing, and will pass them on to the probation officer. If they don't feel a meeting would be possible within a reasonable time, they will say so; if that happens they will have to ask you whether that is the end of the idea, or whether you would accept an approach from Andrew Steel at some later date. But that doesn't have to be decided now!

I'm sorry not be able to bring you a clear-cut answer — it's almost worse than bringing bad news! But if you feel the time has come to set a date, I will pass it on — perhaps it would give them something to work to.

In December, the prison contacted Martin to say that they felt that Andrew Steel still was not ready for a meeting. I wrote to say that if a meeting could not be arranged by the end of June 1992, I would withdraw my request. If he wanted to meet me subsequently, I would respond according to how I felt at that time.

Chapter Ten
Getting to know Micheal on Death Row

BY NOW, Micheal Richard and I had been exchanging letters for a year. He had been delighted to hear of Christopher's birth and asked often for news of how he was progressing.

We had discussed world events, and as the Gulf War came to an end he wrote:

I'm glad the war is almost over, so that it will be peace and the killing will stop, because I feel that killing for oil is wrong, but my opinion doesn't matter and I have no one to share it with . . . Well that's not right because I have you to share my all and that's more than I could ask for in this life. It has been freezing outside and most of the time it's colder in here than outside and to keep warm I have to stay in bed all day, so I haven't been doing that much in the last few weeks except a lot of sleeping.

LifeLines advises correspondents not to ask for information about why a pen friend is on Death Row, so I didn't know how Micheal had come to be there — whether he had killed someone or had been wrongly convicted. He sent me a poem he had written:

Far away sounds behind prison walls
Tiny little rooms and very long halls
I look around to see into each new face
just to find the words to say how much
I hate this painful place.

No use in pretending you are happy
when you know it is a lie.

No use asking the same questions, when
you know the reason why ...
When I had it good I wanted more ... not
really realizing what was really in store.
Now my greed finds me behind prison walls
and I've realized that I couldn't have it all.

This was the first indication that he had done something that led to him being imprisoned, and that he had accepted that he was at fault.

He started signing himself 'Son'. What a cheek! was my first reaction. Biologically it would have been possible for me to have a child at nineteen, but my thoughts at that time had been far from marriage, let alone having a child. However, it did set our relationship in a context, and as his mother had died in 1990, I could see that he might want to see me as a kind of substitute.

Gradually, information about his family emerged. He had three sisters, Ruth, Betty and Pat, and a half-brother, Scott. Pat wrote to him occasionally, but he didn't hear from other members of the family. He was philosophical about this:

Sometimes I think it was best that we weren't that close to each other because now the pain that I've caused them isn't that bad and I know I wouldn't have accepted the handouts that would have been offered me just because I was their little brother and not because they loved me for who I was.

Micheal had two children, a son, Li'l Mike, and a daughter, Doreen, but he hadn't seen them for many years. He sent me photographs of them, two good-looking youngsters. The photographs were taken outside white-painted houses with verandas, surrounded by trees and wide lawns.

Later, he sent me a photograph of himself with the mother

of his children. He is dressed in a long black leather jacket and blue jeans. It is difficult to see his face clearly because he is wearing a baseball cap and the sun is shading his face.

I told Micheal about my attempt to meet Andrew Steel and explained that I was struggling to find a way to forgive him. I had already told Micheal about the trial and the comment of one our nieces: 'I needed to see that he was sorry, and he wasn't.' His response was much fuller than I expected:

Mother dear, I'm sure that Ruth wouldn't want you to become a victim because of her death. I'm not a philosopher, but I can understand your pain and accept your feeling, but until you let go of the guilt that you have given yourself, you will never be able to forgive the young man who caused Ruth's death and it will eat at your whole being and cause you constantly to blame yourself and I know that's not good because you will slowly die from the inside.

Mother dear, you have to give it to God and ask him to show you the way to forgive this man within yourself first and then only will you be able to forgive this man, but something deep down inside of you will always cause you pain, whenever you think of Ruth. I know that all so well, because every time I hear a song that I knew my Mother liked, it brings tears to my eyes and I stop whatever I'm doing for a while.

You will never forget what he did to your loving Ruth, but you will forgive him in your own time and the first step of forgiving him was the appearing of me in your life and yes life does take many unexpected turns. The true unconditional love that you are freely giving me is part of your forgiveness to yourself . . . . I know I will never be able to fill that aching void that you must endure each day, but God wanted us to build a new foundation that will help you as well as myself to accept our loss and still live a very positive and full life.

Lesley, the reason that the two parties most affected are kept apart is to make the offender more of a monster to the victims and he will never know the almost unbearable pain he has caused the family of the victim and they will never get to know him as a person ... but that is the way that society keeps a hold on most of the people that don't know any better and believes everything that is on tv. Mother you will have to let God express your forgiveness to the young man in his own way but you must forgive yourself. The statement that your niece made was wrong and you shouldn't let that influence or affect you in any way whatsoever, because it is very confusing for the victim's family, because she can't have any idea of what was going on in that young man's head.

Micheal was right about not having any idea of how Andrew Steel felt; he had sat very still throughout most of the trial. The only point at which he did more than change his position during the long hours was when his head dropped lower and lower during the pathologist's evidence.

Was I feeling guilty and in need of forgiveness for what had happened to Ruth? I did wonder whether we should have been more involved in the choice of the people who shared the house, or whether we should have warned her about being too willing to take on other people's worries. Ruth was a very independent young woman and wouldn't have taken kindly to our 'interference'; she was also a loving and giving person, and we were proud of her for these very attributes. What kind of society would it be if people reached out to ask for help and were rejected because of the fear of things going wrong? Who could have foreseen that the dull suburban street, so typical of inter-war housing developments, would be the scene for her death? And yet, and yet ... I was her mother and I hadn't been there to protect her, and if I had encouraged her to come home in January she would still be alive. Yes, I had felt and did feel guilt, so Micheal was right that there was that to face as well as finding a way to forgive Andrew Steel.

He was also right that people who commit extreme crimes are usually presented as monsters. This isn't the truth; what they have done is monstrous, but this isn't the whole of their being. Some offenders excuse themselves by saying that if you are a monster, you do monstrous things. People who haven't committed crimes are provided with a convenient dumping ground for the 'bad' parts of themselves by denying that everyone has the capacity to harm others.

Micheal stopped short of saying whether he had caused similar suffering, but he acknowledged the common ground we shared following the death of his mother.

For his birthday in August, I embroidered him a small card with the red, white and blue zigzag airmail symbols making a border and featuring the American and United Kingdom flags and a birthday greeting. He wasn't allowed to have it, but the mail-room staff member on duty that day did show it to him before taking it away. I asked the Texas co-ordinator for LifeLines why Micheal couldn't keep his birthday card. She said it was because I might have impregnated the fabric with drugs. Texas seems to have the harshest death-row regime: nothing but letters, cards and photographs may be sent. In his next letter, he told me:

> I was a little unhappy around my birthday and when I only received one card and nothing from my family that's in the United States, and that one that I did receive was very special and was made by hands just for me, meant so much to me and when I couldn't keep it, that just broke my heart and I was very upset with my family and then with myself for about two weeks. I will stop with this self pity, because I'm the one' dislikes being pitied by anyone and here I am doing it to myself.

I wished that I had checked before sending the card. It had highlighted the lack of other cards he wanted so much, and then he had to endure the frustration of not being able to have it. At least we were lucky that the guard on duty had taken it to show him.

Later, Micheal arranged for the card to be sent to his sister, Pat, for safekeeping, and he sent me a yellow form headed: 'Correspondence/Contraband Denial Form'. The reason given for denial was: 'Contains contraband in violation of Rule 3.9.1.8 – Homeage card denied – uninspectable, no other contents.'

Chapter Eleven
Changes in work, a birth and discovering more about Death Row

NINETEEN NINETY-TWO started with a sudden change from not having enough to occupy myself to constant pressure from work. I was still doing assignments for the management consultancy and had also started a part-time job with a charity working from home. As the stresses increased, I found that I was having difficulty sleeping, menopausal symptoms became more intrusive, and the long-standing arthritis in my neck, arms and hands flared up painfully and more often and spread to my knees. It was clear that I had to make some changes.

One of the first changes was to seek some external help. In April, I started seeing a counsellor twice a month. I said to her firmly that although it was only just over two years since Ruth had died, that wasn't my major reason for deciding to see her. What was it about? I wasn't clear about what I was looking for, but a strong element was trying to find new directions for my life. I was having difficulty in accepting that Vic was not going to discuss his feelings about Ruth's death and did not want me to raise the subject. He was as kind as ever and gave me a lot of support in the new job, taking on the accounting and setting up the computer systems. We still got on very well, but it was at a more superficial level with the great gap left in not talking about Ruth.

*

In May, we had a very happy family occasion to share when

our granddaughter, Marianne, was born. There was a sense of *déjà vu* when we saw her for the first time. She looked very like Catherine as a new-born, with a mass of dark hair. She had been given the second name of Ruth. I wondered if Catherine felt that using her sister's name might comfort her and us. I hoped it wouldn't place any expectations on Marianne to be anyone but herself.

*

Later in the year, I attended a LifeLines conference in London. I looked forward to meeting other people who corresponded with prisoners on Death Row, and to hearing the speaker, Marie Deans from the United States.

Marie spoke powerfully of the brutalising effect of the death penalty on all who are involved in it: the prisoners, the guards, the families, the politicians and American society in general. She described the sensory deprivation endured by prisoners on the Row: the harsh white walls, artificial lighting, poor ventilation, hard surfaces that resonate with harsh sounds. She said:

> The death penalty is an evil that destroys the people on Death Row, their families and their friends. It is an evil that causes decent, ordinary human beings to horribly mistreat other human beings. An evil that reaches out from its vortex and touches us all.

In the discussion that followed her talk, she urged people in Britain to do what they could to inform Americans that the death penalty had not been used in the United Kingdom since 1965, or in other parts of Europe for many years.

At the conference, Jan Arriens' book *Welcome to Hell* was launched. It contains powerful, harrowing testimonies from people on Death Row about the reasons why they were on the Row and about their lives. I couldn't cope with reading it straight through, but tackled it chapter by chapter over a period of some weeks. It confirmed and expanded the accounts that Micheal had given of his life on Death Row.

I wrote to tell him of the impact made on me by the LifeLines conference and Jan's book. Micheal wrote back:

From your letter I gather that you got an ear full of what we have to live through each day, but I try to only think of the things that will help me to better myself and not dwell on the pain that I have to endure each day of my life. My day to day life is very simple and not really much to talk about. First my cell is a lot bigger than some of the other inmates and that is because I live on H wing and it was built for more than one person and since this is Death Row we have to live alone most of the time and that is good because if you have someone living with you and get some bad news from home and you want to be alone it's very hard if you can't. I want to live alone because I've always been a loner and in this position I don't think I could have a cell mate because it's too much pain that we live under and it just wouldn't work.

Lesley, the food is really bad and sometimes is cold when you receive it and I don't eat that much of it, because I can't eat just anything and just seeing it made me sick. I will get you a photo of myself from one of my sisters if I can.

I want you to know that you won't be alone on Xmas, because I'll be with you in my heart and mind and will sing to you from here and in my heart I know you will feel the joy of my singing and will be very happy because you will know that I truly love and wish you and your family the best in the world.

Occasionally, Micheal would mention that he had meetings with lawyers and that he had been working on his case. Then came the news that his case was in the Criminal Court of Appeals but hadn't yet been ruled on.

Micheal had been able to get some art materials, and he sent me some handkerchiefs he had decorated with drawings that were coloured in and with typed or written texts. He demonstrated real skill in his draughtsmanship. One handkerchief that he sent to me for Easter 1992 had the text from Corinthians:

> Love is patient
> Love is kind
> It does not envy, it does not boast, it is not proud
> It is not rude, it is not self-seeking, it is not easily angered,
> It keeps no record of wrong.
> Love does not delight in evil, but rejoices with the truth
> It always protects, always trusts, always hopes,
>   always perseveres.

From time to time, he mentioned the impact of the executions, which took place in Huntsville. 'My spirits have been very low these last few days because of the execution of Billy White and the fact that he didn't tell his family about the execution date.' 'The executions here have really picked up and everyone is wondering if they are next so things have been very difficult around here these last four months, because they have executed six so far this year and have about thirteen more with execution dates this month.'

Just before Christmas 1992, Micheal was visited by two of his sisters, Ruth and Pat. He was delighted to see them, and I was delighted when I received two Polaroid photos of him. He had told me he had made some clocks and wanted to send them to me. In one of the photographs, he is holding the clocks, which are mounted on background pictures of horses. In the second, he is crouching against a plain brick wall, sunglasses nestling in the V of his collarless shirt. His hair is fiercely cropped, clearly showing the structure of his face. It is a strong, handsome face, looking relaxed and at ease as he smiles at the sister taking the photographs.

Towards the end of 1992, Micheal told me that he had a new LifeLines pen friend called Leanne. He sent me her address and telephone number, suggesting that I might contact her; he had given her my address and telephone number. I did contact Leanne, and wrote to let Micheal know that we had been in touch. I said that I was pleased for him that he had another pen friend, but had to confess to a twinge of jealousy. He was very amused by this.

Chapter Twelve

A newspaper article leads to conflict

IN JANUARY 1993, our grandson Christopher was two years old. In February, James Bulger, a toddler from Liverpool, was taken from a shopping centre by two older children, who later killed him. His pictures and pictures of his parents, Denise and Ralph, were everywhere, and the fuzzy video from the shopping centre was played and replayed on the television. Surely no one with the experience of coping with a lively two-year-old could fail to be caught up in speculating that their child, too, could disappear in an instant.

A journalist friend telephoned me to ask if I could help her with an article she had been commissioned to write for the *Independent*. She wanted to interview a number of people whose children had been murdered, and to draw out any experiences that might help the Bulger family.

On the following day, Catherine, the children and my mother came to lunch with me, and we decided to get the supermarket shopping done. My mother offered to look after the children while Catherine and I went to get the groceries. I told Catherine about the interview as we walked up and down the aisles and asked if she thought I should tell my mother. On balance, she felt it was best to say nothing, as my mother didn't read the *Independent*, and as our married surnames were different it was unlikely any of her neighbours would make the connection.

However, when we returned home, someone from the *Independent* rang asking for photographs of Ruth to include with the article, which was due to be published the next day.

They would be sending a courier that afternoon to pick them up. My mother heard my side of the conversation, so I told her what had happened.

The article was published the next day, a Thursday. It included a quote from the interview: 'Mrs Moreland recalls the sense of bewilderment she felt when the police told her the name of the man they had arrested. "But I don't know anything about him and that torments me still – not knowing what kind of person he is or anything about him."'

My mother phoned me mid-morning, sounding upset, and said she wanted me to go up and see her on Sunday, as she had done something that she thought would help me. My heart sank with foreboding, but I agreed to her suggestion. I knew it was highly likely to be something to do with her writing to Andrew Steel. I had known about this since the autumn of 1991, but had not let her know of my contact with the prison chaplain who had revealed that she had been in touch.

I decided not to wait until Sunday, put on my coat and set off on the half-hour walk to her home. When she opened the door, she said, 'You couldn't wait.' We went into the sitting room and she showed me an envelope stuffed with letters. She wanted me to sit down there and then and read the letters in front of her. I said that I wouldn't do that and if she wanted me to read anything, she could give me the letters and I would read them in my own time, in my own home. She said the letters included one from Andrew Steel and handed the envelope to me.

I told her that what she had done was wrong and that she had possibly blocked the careful negotiations I had been going through to arrange a meeting with Andrew Steel. She was upset and started to cry. I said I would come back on Sunday to discuss things at greater length when we were both calmer.

I walked quickly down the curving road away from my mother's maisonette, carrying the brown manila envelope with 'On Her Majesty's Service' and 'HOME OFFICE S.4.C' printed across the top. As soon as I was out of sight, I took out the bundle of letters. I could see that some of the letters were copies of those written by my mother and that there were letters from people at the prison. There was also an envelope addressed to my mother in handwriting I didn't recognise, and a cutting from an Enfield newspaper about the outcome of the trial. Incongruously, there was another envelope that contained a photograph of my mother with Christopher when he was a few months old.

In date order, the contents read as follows.

COPY OF LETTER TO MATT MILLER FROM MY MOTHER:

30th October 1991

Thank you so very much for the prison name passed on via the solicitors, the local library will be able to give me the address.

I know your viewpoint is different to mine, but it must be affected to some extent by your close contact with the criminal world.

While I know that punishment for wrongdoing must be exacted, it should not preclude some effort to save the soul of the wrongdoer.

When I think about the concentration of criminals in prisons, I think about the concentration of evil that must ensue, how very difficult that must be for prison officers to contend with.

At one time I thought islands could be used for various forms of villainy — all the thieves on one — they could steal from each other until it dawns on them that no-one wins, I wonder if it would work or am I being naïve?

I keep very busy (considering my age). I started going to the local primary school last year to listen to 9 year old children read and correct their pronunciation etc — two 1 hour sessions a week, I enjoy it very much and the children's teacher says it's a great help.

My great grandson is a joy, he really lightens our darkness, it's lovely to see Lesley and Vic with him. So you see, we do not hug our sorrow overmuch, like most folk we get on with our lives.

Again, many thanks for making time to help me.

FROM MY MOTHER TO THE PRISON GOVERNOR:

October 1991
Enclosed is a letter I wrote to a man who is at present in your care. He was convicted of murdering my youngest granddaughter, Ruth Moreland at her home in Enfield, Middx. in February 1990. I believe he would be 22 or 23 years old.

I write because I believe that someone who takes life harms them-selves in the deepest sense more than the victim. I am not a 'do gooder' or a 'churchy' person, but know that the soul is the most important part of one.

I know very little about him and his family, but leave it to you to judge if my letter would help him.

Forgive me if I add to your burden of duties, I hope you understand why I do.

COPY OF LETTER FROM MY MOTHER TO ANDREW STEEL:

5th November 1991
Although I have started writing this letter to you, I am not sure that I will send it. If I do, it will be because I feel you should know what the consequences of your act were. Ruth's death and the way she died, broke our hearts, she was indeed dearly beloved.

No, she was not perfect, who is on this earth? But she was a loving, caring person and an essential part of our family.

The last time I saw Ruth was on the Wednesday before she died, I was the last one in the family to see her alive.

She had phoned to ask if she could come for a soupy lunch, something we used to enjoy together from time to time. Ruth was upset about having to tell Tom that their relationship was over, she was a very tender hearted girl.

I treasured our growing friendship because circumstances prevented me from seeing much of Ruth and her sister Catherine while they were growing up.

We, Ruth and I, were planning a very special 50th birthday present for her mother (June 1990) and had visited a local artist together to commission a painting of bluebells, a favourite flower, but Ruth never saw the picture, which wasn't ready until April.

It is so very hard for me to write all this and there is so much more I could tell you about Ruth and my family — an ordinary family.

I want you to know that I do not hate you, and that I do not feel you are an evil person.

I would like to think you could learn from whoever is able to help you reshape your life, you will still be young when you are freed. I hope your family are in touch with you and giving you support.

If you are allowed, perhaps you would like to write to me sometime, I feel strongly that Ruth would understand and approve.

No-one apart from necessary intermediaries, will know that I have written to you.

FROM THE PRISON GOVERNOR TO MY MOTHER:

8th November 1991
Thank you for your letter of the 5th November 1991. I do not know Andrew Steel well but see him around the prison fairly regularly. I have studied his record to see how he is settling down.

I feel your letter needs handling with care and I will ask his Wing Manager to sit down and discuss it with him, rather than just give it to

him. Hopefully, he will be able to use this contact constructively, but
that decision has to be his.

Thank you for taking the trouble to write. I know how difficult it
must have been having lost your granddaughter so tragically. If I can
help further, please let me know.

LETTER FROM THE PRISON PROBATION OFFICER
TO MY MOTHER:

29th November 1991
The Governor asked me to discuss your letter with Andrew Steel who I
know and with whom I have regular contact. He now has your letter and
we have talked about it on a number of occasions.

He is emotionally very fragile and has some difficulty in his efforts
to come to terms not only with actions of that tragic day but latterly with
your letter. We are continuing to work, helping him to gain insight and
understanding into his actions and the dreadful repercussions of his
behaviour. He is remorseful and appreciates the loss you have suffered
but remains unable to contact you directly and has asked me to write to
you. Hopefully one day he will be able to express his feelings to you
himself.

For myself, I understand the trauma you must have suffered and the
effort to work through your own deep sense of loss. I am grateful that I
have had the opportunity to discuss this with Andy who in time, I am
sure will appreciate your act of kindness towards him.

DRAFT LETTER FROM MY MOTHER TO THE PRISON
PROBATION OFFICER:

January 1992
Thank you for your letter. I am sorry for the delayed reply.
Please tell Andy I understand his inability to write to me as yet, I

can appreciate the adjustments he is having to make, the loss of freedom of life in prison on top of coming to terms with his action, it is a lot to cope with.

I know very little of what life is like in prison, only programmes on TV like the one recently shown of Christmas at Strangeways Prison, which can only give just an inkling.

Does his family keep in touch with him, I do hope so, even though they too have had to cope with their trauma. Also is he able to watch TV and listen to the radio?

I have not told my daughter (Lesley) that I am in touch with him through you, I know she, like Ruth, would understand and approve, but as I am uncertain of her husband's reaction, I will not burden her with the possibility of having to keep such a secret from him, also I would not wish to hurt him, he is like a son to me. My own son is mentally handicapped and lives in a small community.

Could you let me know Andy's birthday date, I would send a card.

My other granddaughter, Catherine had a son on Jan 7th 1991, he is such a joy to our family, he has lightened our darkness.

Thank you very much for your understanding letter, and for sending it in a plain envelope, any possible publicity would be too upsetting, especially as the police protected us from the media, they were so good to us.

LETTER FROM MY MOTHER TO ANDREW STEEL:

8th December 1992
You see, I have not forgotten you, in fact I think of you quite often and hope you have adjusted to your life in prison.

I now have two great grandchildren, a boy and a girl, they bring great joy to myself and my family.

Also I go to the local primary school to help children with their reading, I enjoy that very much, they become my friends and life goes on.

I would still be pleased to hear from you if you feel like writing to me. *Tell me about your interests, do you like sport, and are you able to watch television or listen to the radio, there are a lot of good programmes if one is selective.*

I have put in a spare label in with this in case you feel like writing to me.

LETTER FROM ANDREW STEEL TO MY MOTHER (ENVELOPE POSTMARKED 15 DECEMBER 1992):

Dear Joy

I received your letter and card! Well joy I don't know what to say it's really hard for me to express myself the way I want to I know deep down your thinking what a horrible guy who has no feelings well Joy if only you knew how sorry I feel for what I have done!

I know I have taken your granddaughter away from you! And if I could turn the clock back I would! Well Joy deep down inside I am a nice guy! And I am sorry for what I have put you and your family through!

Well Joy I have still got your last letter and I will always keep it. Oh Joy sorry for taking so long to write back to you! But it's just that I haven't got over what has happened yet!

I'm always feeling really guilty for what I have done and sometimes I can't get to sleep and I'm up all night crying and thinking so please try to understand that I'm really sorry! Well Joy, I would like to say I appreciate you writing to me for I know it's hard for you to write to me! Well Joy I don't know when I will write again so I'm saying thank you for trying to understand and writing to me!

And take care of yourself okay!

Bye bye Joy

It didn't take long to read through the contents as I walked, then stumbled, towards my home. I was shaking with fury and outrage and gritting my teeth so that I didn't cry. I was nearly home when I met someone I have known for a number of years through a local group. She took one look at me and said 'Are you all right?' I said I was feeling upset and would she mind if I didn't stop to catch up on news. I would phone her later. She held my arm and said she would 'walk me home'. I couldn't bring myself to say, 'Please don't', and all the way to the house I was wondering how I would manage not to invite her in and how I could hang on and not cry before getting indoors.

The letters added nothing to my knowledge of Andrew Steel. His letter showed that he was still immersed in self-pity. But the dominant cause of my rage was my mother's assumption that Ruth and I would approve of what she had done. She was wrong as far I was concerned, and I felt no one had the right to make any assumptions about Ruth's views.

It was fortunate that I was seeing the counsellor the next day. I was already regretting telling my mother that she was wrong to have contacted the prison. I had held back from telling her that I was trying to meet Andrew Steel, so we were both at fault. She was, as we all were, still very affected by Ruth's death. The discussion with the counsellor explored the need to respect the rights of everyone involved. She encouraged me to stand up for my rights as Ruth's mother and to ensure that my mother realised that she had acted inappropriately, perhaps by asking her to consider how she would have felt if our positions had been reversed. I rehearsed with the counsellor what I could say on Sunday that would express my feelings clearly and yet not cause a total fracture in the often difficult relationship between my mother and myself.

My mother looked at me warily when I arrived. I had a sheet of paper with notes on so that I could be sure of saying all that I needed to.

I started by saying that what she had done had upset me a lot, but I understood this had not been her intention. She said she had felt suicidal after I left on Thursday (she had threatened suicide many times over many years). I responded by saying that this was emotional blackmail and I wasn't going to take it — the first time I had ever responded to her so firmly. After half an hour of discussion, she still seemed not to understand why I was so upset. We reached an impasse. She then suggested that perhaps it would be a good idea if we had a break from each other. I agreed, but said she still needed some support, though not from me. We discussed the possibility of her going to see the family GP, who was well known to and trusted by both of us.

After returning home, I realised that we had not discussed who was to make the first approach or how long such a break should be. I phoned my cousin, Carole, who knew about and understood the difficulties of my relationship with my mother. She offered to contact my mother the next day. Midweek, a letter arrived from my mother.

25th February
How fortunate we are to have Carole to turn to in our need, she rang me on Monday, and in that quiet, calm way she has, talked me through the present trauma.

I did not realise at the time (of writing to the prison) that I was stealing what was rightfully yours, one's emotions can cloud one's thinking.

For you to continue caring about and for me the way you did, so generously, in spite of your hurt and anger, has increased even more my respect and admiration for you, as well as the very special love I have had for you since the day you were born.

This has made me realise and understand more your feelings about my action.

My tears and momentary suicidal feelings were an expression of my anguish that I had hurt you both so much.

I hope you can find it in your heart to forgive me? Would you like our next meeting to be over a cup of coffee in a local café?

With love, Mum

I phoned and arranged to see her the next day. I took the packet of letters with me and told her I had made photocopies. We didn't talk much about what had happened between us.

Chapter Thirteen
Progress towards a meeting

In March 1994, Vic and I went on a ten-day coach holiday to Spain. The weather was just as we like it — warm enough to walk around outdoors in summer clothes.

In Cordoba, we visited a small palace surrounded by exquisite courtyard gardens, one with a wall of wisteria at its full peak of pale-lilac scented racemes, with tubs of deep-purple petunias in front. We planned to make a courtyard garden on a smaller scale at home.

The holiday had its moments of humour. While we were waiting to go into the mosque in Cordoba, the local guide told something about its history. A group of secondary-school-age children were nearby, making quite a noise with their chattering. The guide remonstrated with their teacher, asking that the group move further away or pipe down. This request was repeated twice without any noticeable decrease in the sound level. Quite suddenly, the guide closed his eyes, thrust his arms skyward in a beseeching gesture and cried, 'I *pray* for the resurrection of Herod!' I laughed as heartily as the rest of the group, and for the first time since Ruth's death the laughter did not turn to tears.

As we boarded the plane to return home, we felt relaxed; we had a store of visual and other sensory memories to give us pleasure for many years to come.

Every seat in the plane had a complimentary copy of the *Evening Standard* on it. 'MURDER! MURDER! MURDER!' shrieked at us as we made our way up the aisle. An IRA bomb in Warrington had killed one child; another was critically injured. Our brief escape had ended and the flight home became an endurance test.

★

Not long after our return, I was contacted by Marian Liebmann, the director of Mediation UK, who had heard of my wish to meet Andrew Steel through Martin Wright of Victim Support. Marian had been approached by someone from Yorkshire Television (YTV) who was researching a programme about the work of the West Yorkshire Probation Service in bringing together offenders and victims of crime. They wanted to interview someone from another area of the country, and Marian had offered to contact me to see if I would be willing to talk to them. I was very interested to hear about this initiative and wanted to find out more. If meetings had been arranged in some parts of the country, it was difficult to see why they couldn't happen elsewhere.

Pat Evans, the researcher, came to see me at my home and said they had been filming for some time, following mediators, victims and offenders as they arranged and held meetings. The scheme was one of four pilots set up by the Home Office, and the West Yorkshire Probation Service was strongly committed to the project.

Later, Jill Nicholls, the producer, also came to see me. She explained that it might take some time for decisions to be made about the final shape of the programme. They were already filming and would carry on for some months to come. I felt I could trust the programme makers, and agreed to consider taking part if they wanted me to do so later in the year.

A letter arrived from Pat in August setting out their proposals for my involvement.

The senior probation officer from Leeds, Peter Johnstone,

had already spoken to probation officers at Gartree Prison where Andrew Steel was now serving his sentence. They were happy for Peter to talk to me and for a film to be made of a session when Peter would brief me about the possible ways to get in touch with Andrew Steel. They hadn't ruled out the possibility of a meeting, but thought it would be some time before it happened.

It was good news that the prison staff were at least not ruling out the possibility of a meeting between Andrew Steel and myself. I wasn't sure how I felt about a film being made of such a meeting – it should be essentially a private encounter. However, I was happy to take part in any project that might demonstrate the value of bringing victims and offenders together, when both parties were willing to meet, and thought perhaps that it might be possible to arrange to be interviewed about the meeting after it had happened – if it did.

A series of rail strikes were planned for the autumn, and one was due on 13 September, the day when filming was to take place in Leeds. I thought it would be rearranged, but instead YTV laid on a chauffeur-driven car and flights to and from Leeds. Another car met me from Leeds airport and I was soon in the YTV offices. There were banks of desks, phones ringing and piles of papers everywhere, from which Pat Evans emerged and introduced me to her colleagues. The rest of the film crew and Jill Nicholls soon arrived, and we set off to a basement in a converted church. The Mediation and Reparation Service used it regularly for mediator training sessions and for meetings between victims and offenders. Although there was no daylight, it was a bright space, even more so once the television filming lights were in position.

Peter Johnstone, the senior probation officer, arrived, full of bonhomie. We sat and ran through the kind of questions that he and the mediator would ask. There were none that I minded answering, but I wanted to ask questions, too, and to get some answers.

Soon filming began with an interview by the mediator. She took me through the sequence of events and asked about my reactions to Ruth's murder and why I wanted to meet Andrew Steel.

Then it was time for the interview with Peter. I was unprepared for what he had to say. He had spoken on the phone to Andrew Steel at Gartree Prison. My reaction was immediate and fierce: I was very angry that he had been able to achieve this so easily. It wasn't *his* life that had been affected; it was that of Ruth's family and friends. I had found the criminal justice system impenetrable and unresponsive to my needs, but Peter had not only spoken to prison staff, he had made direct contact with Andrew Steel. Peter then said that Andrew Steel was willing to meet me. Despite my shock, I had to admit that this was a major step forward.

I asked Peter what I should do next. He outlined the new rights that formed part of the Victims' Charter, published in 1990. These included the new duties placed on the probation service, making them responsible for the victims of serious crime as well as for the offenders. The home probation officer of the offender now had a responsibility to contact the victim's family. The home probation officer is based in the offender's home area — that is, where they were living when they committed their offence. This probation officer's role was to maintain contact with the offender and their family throughout the entire sentence and afterwards, while prison probation officers would change as long-term-sentence offenders were moved to less secure prisons during the course of their sentence. However, I couldn't work out how the home probation officer would even have been able to trace who we were. We formed no part of the official records, and Ruth had lived at a different address from ours. We might have moved to another part of the country in the meantime, and then how would they have traced us?

★

The work that the West Yorkshire Probation Service had done with victims and offenders had established that three pre-conditions needed to be in place before any contact could be planned. They were:

—That the offender must have accepted responsibility for their crime.

—That any contact or meeting should be safe for all parties, physically and psychologically.

—That both the offender and the victim had willingly agreed to be in touch.

These seemed very sensible, and now I knew that the first and third conditions were in place in my own case.

★

Peter had found out the name and address of Andrew Steel's home probation officer and said I should write to him to request a meeting.

The next day, I wrote to the home probation officer, Jim Fotheringham, asking if I could meet with him to discuss the implications of the Victims' Charter and to seek his help in arranging a meeting with Andrew Steel. I also mentioned the possibility of YTV's interest in filming such a meeting, though I was concerned that this might complicate progress.

His response suggested meeting either at my home or at his office in late October. However, on 18 October, he wrote again to say that he needed to consult with colleagues and to talk to Andrew Steel before he could agree to our meeting being filmed, and therefore the meeting would be postponed.

Early in November, he wrote again suggesting a meeting for 23 November, when Eric Scott, Andrew Steel's prison probation officer at Gartree Prison, would also be present. Jim had now talked to Andrew Steel, who did not want any filming to take place. I couldn't go to a meeting on that date as I already had four work commitments which could not be rearranged. I advised Jill and Pat that it wouldn't be possible to film; they were disappointed, but pleased for me that through their contacts I had got further than before in trying to meet Andrew Steel.

So, third time lucky, the date was reset for 7 December 1994. It was quite a daunting prospect to be going to see two people whose professional responsibilities were, I felt, primarily for Andrew Steel, and the meeting was to be held on their territory. I asked my friend Roma if she would be willing to come with me. She agreed and we arranged to meet for lunch at her home before going to the probation office in North London.

Roma and I discussed how the meeting might proceed. I thought it would be best to take the initiative and ask the probation officers if they had any previous experience of working with victims of crime or of implementing the Victims' Charter. If they hadn't, then we would be starting from the same basis, and if they had, their response would give some indication of their attitudes.

I had had plenty of time to think about why I wanted to meet Andrew Steel, and ran through the key points with Roma before we left to make the short journey to the probation offices.

First, I wanted to find out more about what kind of person Andrew Steel was and what had been going on his life before he killed Ruth. I had never heard his name before he was charged with her murder. Because he had exercised his right not to give evidence at the trial, there had been no opportunity to form any first-hand opinions about him. The police had told us that he had a history of violence towards women and that he had broken a previous girlfriend's arm. They had tried to get some of the women to give evidence, but they were too frightened. The police had painted a picture of a young man whose behaviour was antisocial; in addition to the violence, he was a thief and drug abuser. At the trial, the defence evidence included information about problems at school: he was bullied; he suffered from asthma. But apart from hearing his response to the charge of murder and acknowledging his identity, we hadn't ever heard him speak.

Second, I wanted to hear from him directly, in his own words, what happened and why he thought he had killed Ruth. I realised that any explanation would be likely to be incomplete and might raise as many questions as it answered. I could see that there were risks involved. He might tough it out or say hurtful things about Ruth. But his action had had a major impact on my life, on all members of my family and many other people, and I felt he owed me an explanation. I recognised that no meeting could take place against his will, and indeed it would have no value if he were coerced into agreeing to it.

I wanted to ask if his family were in touch with him, if they were supportive, and how they were coping.

I wanted to know if he was getting any help and if he had any plans for when he left prison. Was he being given any training or educational support? My greatest fear was that he might be released and then kill or harm someone else if he didn't know about the impact of his act or left prison without the necessary skills to establish a new, non-violent life.

And finally, I wanted him to know that despite our great and ongoing grief about Ruth's death and the manner of her death, our lives were continuing constructively.

This was my agenda for the meeting with the probation officers. While I couldn't 'act' a part, I wanted to present myself as calm and reasonable. What I didn't want to share at this meeting was my hope that I if met Andrew Steel, I might be able to say that I could forgive him for killing Ruth.

The probation offices are approached by a steep climb up a flight of white steps. I was very glad to have Roma with me as we arrived at the front door, chilled by an icy wind blowing down the long straight road, to ring the bell and wait to hear the lock being released. I was feeling nervous and also curious to find out how we would be received. The receptionist took us upstairs, then along corridors formed by flimsy panelling to Jim Fotheringham's office. It was a long, thin room with the door in the centre of its length. To the left, there were filing cabinets and a desk with neat stacks of files and papers; to the right, some upholstered chairs surrounded a low table. Introductions were made and we were offered tea or coffee.

Once the mugs were on the table, I immediately asked if either of the probation officers had worked with victims before. The answer was 'no' for both of them. I grinned and said, 'Well, that means we are all novices,' and they smiled back at me.

The two men were very different. Jim was tall, slender, his speech measured and careful, his posture and stillness suggesting a reflective personality. Eric was shorter and stockier, gesturing as he spoke rapidly and energetically.

I ran through my 'agenda' and handed over a small folder of photographs of Ruth taken from the training video within weeks of her death and, at the back, a photograph of her as a bridesmaid to Catherine, with a lock of her hair facing it.

Eric explained that the Victims' Charter had come into being in 1991 and that it was still early days for its implementation. He was a seconded officer working with life-sentence prisoners. His job was to maintain links, write reports and assess risk potential, progress during sentence and future plans for prisoners.

The prison had established a therapeutic community in 1993, using a segregation wing that had been left empty. Prisoners could volunteer to be part of the community. Those who applied tended to be the ones who wanted to gain insight into their behaviour. Each applicant was assessed before being admitted to the community. The preconditions included having at least an average IQ, no prevailing mental illness and not to be taking any psychotropic drugs. Each member had to sign a contract agreeing not to drink alcohol, take drugs, have sex or be violent. If the contract was broken, they would immediately be removed from the community.

Andrew Steel had applied to join the community and had been accepted; he was one of seven men in his group. Eric had met with him three times a week at group and individual meetings.

Eric said: 'Jim and I find it difficult to know how to respond to you; our training and experience is totally in working with offenders. I have to consider where Andrew Steel is in his therapy and the needs of the other people in the therapeutic community.'

I asked how Andrew Steel was faring in the community. Eric said, 'He's making considerable efforts to understand himself, his offence, how it came about and his previous lifestyle.'

Eric confirmed that Andrew Steel had willingly agreed to meet me. He'd even said that he could see that he received plenty of help while victims' families had none. We were both looking for answers to the same questions.

Eric saw his task as preparing Andrew Steel and myself for a meeting. Andrew Steel had wanted to write to me for some time but was frightened to do so. Eric believed that he was genuinely sorry for killing Ruth. It had taken him a long time to get past denial and blocking out his actions. It had been difficult during the early part of his sentence to get him to remember anything, to get any sense out him. He was in a prison culture where the first priority was survival; and this fostered denial. The therapeutic community challenged this and had removed some of the blocks, so that Andrew Steel had been able to express more of his fears towards me and about himself and his family.

Jim sat quietly, contributing little to the discussion, but I was very conscious of a presence that had great integrity. Roma was taking notes – this had been agreed previously – and occasionally prompting me.

I was asked if I considered the meeting to be part of my healing process. I said yes, but it was more than that: it was to obtain information that only Andrew Steel could provide; to get some idea of what kind of person he was; to find out what had happened in his life that could have led to him killing Ruth.

Eric agreed that Andrew Steel needed to be made aware of the impact of his act. Eric could see the benefits for Andrew Steel and for me, and he said he would do everything he could to arrange a meeting.

He would need to confer with colleagues at the prison, and thought that a further meeting would be necessary to discuss arrangements. If so, it would be easier if the second meeting took place near the prison.

Jim explained that the role of the home probation officer was to provide an ongoing contact throughout a life-sentence prisoner's time in prison. Towards the end of the sentence, the home probation officer had the responsibility of contacting the victim's family to find out whether they had any views about restrictions being placed on where the offender could live. These views would be taken into consideration, but not necessarily put into effect. This wasn't something that concerned me unduly, as Andrew Steel's family lived quite a distance from our home and it was possible that we might have moved by the time he was released. Jim acknowledged that many probation officers were wary about contacting victims' families – they were unsure of the response they might encounter.

Andrew Steel had found it more difficult to contact me because I wasn't vengeful towards him; he found this difficult to understand. It would have been easier for him if I had expressed anger towards him. He was wary of being subjected to a barrage of information that he would find hurtful, and Eric would need to prepare him for what might prove to be a painful experience. Eric said I shouldn't hold back from whatever I wanted to say.

We discussed where any letter that Andrew Steel might write to me should be sent, and agreed that it would be sent care of Jim, so that my home address would not be revealed.

The meeting ended in a friendly way, with handshakes all round. Roma was going to take me to a nearby station, and we offered Eric a lift.

During the short journey to the station, I thanked Roma for coming with me and she gave me the notes she had taken at the meeting. We agreed to contact each other the next day when we had had time to absorb the experience of meeting the two probation officers.

★

Eric and I walked into the station. I was travelling north, he south, so we would be leaving from different platforms. As we reached the stairs to his platform, he suddenly asked, 'Can I give you a hug?' We stood and hugged; this felt really warm and supportive, and sustained me during the journey home.

When Roma and I spoke the next day, we agreed that the meeting had gone well. It was difficult to gain any sense of a time scale, but now the process was under way.

Shortly afterwards, I received a letter from Eric.

Jim and I felt that the meeting was constructive as a first stage to establishing, at least, some common ground for a working relationship and for moving forward.

I have given Andy some feedback albeit without pulling too many punches. Nonetheless, he wishes to press ahead and has asked me to tell you that he does intend to write. For my part, I am pleased to have met you and I do hope that in the final analysis, for you and for Andy, some sense can be gained from the senseless.

I wondered if a letter would arrive before the end of the year, and watched the post each day looking for Jim's distinctive handwriting on an envelope.

Chapter Fourteen
A letter from Andrew Steel; delays in arranging the meeting

MOST OF JANUARY 1995 went by before a letter from Andrew Steel arrived. It was dated the eighteenth of January but, as agreed, had been sent to Jim who had then forwarded it to me. It read:

Dear Lesley

I didn't know how to start this letter so perhaps I could start by telling you a little bit about myself. I was born in (London, Hackney) I lived with my mother, father, sister up to the age of 16 years old then I left home to start my own family. but things didn't work out for me and my girlfriend. We had a little boy! We was both 18 years old and to immature to understand what big responsibility we had taken on with that the relationship ended.

Then I started drinking and taking drugs. Well time went on and I started going to partys that how I got to meet Tom, the guy ruth was living with. Me and Tom got to be really good friends! Well in time I ended up going my way and so did Tom. then we both got back in touch and started going pubs then Tom told me he was going with a girl named Ruth and that he was sharing a house with ruth. And asked me if I would like to meet her. because they was having a party. Well thats how I got to meet ruth. and to get to know someone like Ruth, nice person well thought of by others proved to be a good friend. Kind and supportive well that makes it hard for us both to understand what happened. Lesley I dont know how to put this because I felt really nervous about writing to you! I was told you really want to know what happened that night well it's to hard to put down on paper and to go into Detail. It's to

*soon for this to happen but in time maybe it will be easier for you and I
to talk it through. Well Eric told me about the meeting you had with
him and Jim my probation officer and I have a lot of trust in them. and I
only hope they can help you and I will do all I can to help you to! I cant
find the words to say how sorry to you and your family because I dont
think sorry is the right words to put. It seems that no words or Actions
could express this properly!*

*Thanks for taking your time to read this letter and please bear with
me and I hope that we can begin to get something out of this and not
wast opportunities!*

Take care of yourself lesley

His description of Ruth as being 'kind and supportive' did
indeed make it hard to understand why he had then attacked
and killed her. I was relieved to see that he thought highly of
the two probation officers. At least we would have that in
common.

I sent a cool reply to his letter, having waited until after
the fifth anniversary of Ruth's death and having hoped that
that by the time I wrote a date for a meeting would have been
arranged:

*Thank you for your letter which I realise must have been a difficult one
for you to write. I have waited to reply until hearing the outcome of Jim
Fotheringham's recent visit to you at the prison about possible dates for
a meeting.*

*It was helpful that you were able to tell me something about your-
self and your life before 1990. I do want you to know that I appreciated
the information you sent me following the meetings you requested with
my friend, Jane, the probation officer at Wormwood Scrubs, in 1991. It
was because you had asked to see her that I felt encouraged to seek a
face to face meeting. Like you, I think we could both benefit from dis-
cussing Ruth's death and its aftermath for us and our families.*

I was pleased to hear that you were offered and have accepted the opportunity to join the therapeutic group at Gartree.

I hope very much that it will not be too long before we are able to meet.

Negotiations now started to arrange a date for a meeting as soon as possible. But weeks went by; Jim had to postpone a visit to the prison to talk to Andrew Steel because of the sickness of a colleague. Then Andrew Steel was transferred to another prison for some weeks so that his family could visit him more easily.

After Jim's visit to the prison in April, he told me that Andrew Steel had again confirmed that he was willing to meet me. He said, 'I owe her that.' This mirrored my own feelings.

Jim also said that Eric wanted to arrange a further meeting and suggested that we travelled together to Leicester in May.

On 4 May, Jim and I arranged to meet at St Pancras. It was a very hot day and the countryside was full of new growth. We talked of many things on the journey to Leicester. Jim enthused about gardening and said he raised lots of annual flowers from seed. 'What are your favourites?' I asked. 'Anything from asters to zinnias,' he replied. He was concerned that the hot weather that day might burn some of his seedlings. When I described one of Vic's hobbies as knotwork, he laughed and said, 'I can just picture it. You knitting and Vic knotting side by side in the evenings!'

We arrived early at Leicester and, having located the meeting venue, backtracked to the shopping centre and spent half an hour in a bookshop browsing and comparing purchases. Returning to the venue, we were shown to a room with ceiling-high glass partitions and closed windows. It was stiflingly hot. The posters were mainly about marriage guidance, and I teased Jim that when people walked by they might think we were a warring couple coming for help.

After a while, Eric arrived and the three of us moved to another room, which, thankfully, was much cooler. As at the meeting in December, Eric asked far more questions than Jim. He seemed anxious and said that the negotiations at the prison were proving tricky. He had to liaise with a lot of people, all of whom wanted to have their views taken into consideration. 'Establishing precedents' was a wearying process. I began to feel alarmed when it seemed that a large group of people wanted to be present at the meeting. This wasn't what I had envisaged at all. We went yet again over my reasons for wanting to meet Andrew Steel. Eric sighed at one point and said, 'I can't get my head around it.' I respected his honesty in saying this, and saw that it was quite a problem for him to be the 'go-between' who had to convince sceptical colleagues. He was working hard to facilitate a course of action which wouldn't have been his own choice in my situation. I sensed also that there were perhaps issues about people wanting to be part of something unusual and that he was having to fend them off.

Jim and I returned to the station. While waiting for the train, I said that I felt as if we had just gone over the same ground as at the December meeting six months before. What had this meeting really been about? Jim agreed, and said he thought that Eric needed to test my resolve and to confirm that I wanted the meeting to go ahead only if Andrew Steel were willing. I could understand this. I had never wanted him to be coerced; only a meeting that we both wanted would have any point or value.

Another letter from Andrew Steel arrived soon after the visit to Leicester:

Dear Lesley

This is just a few lines to say thanks for the letter that you sent me!
At the time you sent the letter I was in another prison.

Sorry I havent wrote back sooner. I had a lot of issues to work on.
Eric came to talk to me a few weeks ago to say that you wanted to meet
me and he gave me some date's for this month (22, 23, 24 May) is the
dates alright for you! Well all we are waiting for is prison headquarters
to say it is alright to have this meeting in this prison. It shouldn't be a
problem. I havent seen Jim Fotheringham yet!

Well again thanks for writing to me. Until I hear or get to meet you
take care of yourself Lesley. I do hope we can get to meet Lesley.

The following week, Jim let me know that the negotiations with 'prison headquarters' meant that a meeting in May would not be possible.

Chapter Fifteen
LifeLines conference

LifeLines holds two conferences each year; the autumn one is held in London and the spring one moves around the country. I had agreed to speak at the conference held in Edinburgh in May 1995 on the theme of 'Victims and Reconciliation'.

The first speaker at the conference was Pat Bane. Pat was the director of an American organisation called Murder Victim's Families for Reconciliation (MVFR). One of her uncles had been murdered some years before, and she and other relatives of murder victims who were against the death penalty had come together to form MVFR.

Pat produced a great deal of evidence to show that the death penalty does not act as a deterrent and brings no comfort to the victims. At one point in her presentation she said, 'There can be no forgiveness without understanding.' That rang a clear bell with me – I didn't understand why Ruth had been killed and whether Andrew Steel had any understanding of what he had done. I was still reflecting on this when it was my turn to speak.

I had taken some slides of Ruth and of Micheal to show the audience. The slide projector wasn't one that I or anyone else there was familiar with, and there were some anxious moments when the first slide got stuck in the projector. For one awful moment, I thought the slides, and their precious images, would be irretrievably damaged. Finally the projector was working smoothly and I was able to give my presentation calmly.

Immediately after lunch, a video interview with Leanne,

Micheal's other LifeLines pen friend, was shown. Leanne had suffered a dreadful attack when she was in her teens and was still suffering physically and emotionally. Despite her injuries, she had seen the man who attacked her as a fellow human being and had been able to forgive him.

The final speaker was Betty Foster. Her son, Chris, was executed in Georgia in December 1993 after seventeen years on Death Row for killing a man when he was seventeen years old. He had been given seven death warrants and six repeals. Chris was executed thirteen days after Betty's husband had died of cancer.

Her last visit to see Chris had a particularly cruel twist. She had been told that she could stay with him until 3.30 p.m. At 3 p.m., the assistant warden came in and said they had another fifteen minutes before she had to leave. She pleaded and the time was restored. But at 3.25 p.m., he returned and insisted that she leave immediately.

LifeLines audiences have been present at many shocking presentations, but this was the first time I had seen so many people openly crying. The sheer inhumanity of Betty's treatment added so much to her suffering – and it went on. She hadn't been able to afford to buy headstones for her husband and her son.

*

Next day, my journey home from Scotland took many hours as the trains were delayed. I sat at Stevenage station waiting for a long time for the next train southwards. There were no staff around, so I went to the upper part of the station and was told there was a notice outside to say that no trains were running south; a bus service was being provided, but I had just missed one. So another long wait, then I got on the bus which trailed around all the villages, as well as stopping at each railway station between Stevenage and London. After a while, I got off the bus and went to Catherine's, got through the door and started crying in her arms. I was absolutely drained and needed to rest before going home. Of all the LifeLines conferences I have attended, Betty Foster's presentation is the one that has left the most enduring mark, and it caused me to think a great deal about Andrew Steel's and Micheal's families.

Chapter Sixteen
An unexpected visit to Texas

IN NOVEMBER 1993, Micheal had been transferred to Houston Prison to await a retrial. Nearly twenty dates had been set and then cancelled, often at very short notice. He had been on a roller coaster of raised and dashed hopes, and his spirits fluctuated accordingly.

One of his attorneys had promised him that he would be released in time for Christmas, but this didn't happen. Another predicted that he would be given a life sentence of thirty to forty years. None of the attorneys stayed around for long. By the summer of 1994, he was still waiting for the retrial to go ahead.

*

In August 1994, the *Sunday Times* wanted to publish an article about LifeLines. Jan Arriens asked me if I would be willing to be interviewed. When the article appeared, I was shocked to see the details of the crime that Micheal had committed. He had killed a woman called Marguerite Dixon who was fifty-three years old. I was now fifty-four. Micheal was pictured full faced, unsmiling – it was the official prison-record photograph.

One of the journalists on the *Sunday Times*, Rebecca Fowler, was working for the *Washington Post* on an exchange scheme. She contacted me to say that she wanted to do an article and would be visiting Micheal in Houston Prison.

Rebecca phoned me soon after her visit, and I was eager to hear her account. It must have been a daunting experience for her to travel alone to Houston and interview Micheal. He was shackled and handcuffed. Prison staff were in the room throughout the interview. She said that she found him to be a mixture of a cheeky adolescent and an adult capable of profound thought. I was amused to hear that she thought Micheal rather vain, as he had a comb in his pocket and wanted me to know that his hair was longer than the photograph used in the *Sunday Times* article.

I hadn't realised that he had not previously had any ongoing contact with a white person; he told Rebecca how important it was to him that our friendship was based on equality. Early in our correspondence, I had sent him a feather dropped by a guinea fowl as it walked in front of me in Kew Gardens. He had treasured this small gift, a soft reminder of the natural world that he missed so much.

*

On 7 June 1995, I had a telephone call from a man called Christopher Goldsmith. He introduced himself as being the lead attorney for Micheal's defence in his retrial. I hadn't known that the retrial had started. The dates had been set and cancelled so often that I hadn't raised my hopes that it would go ahead on the date Micheal told me had been set for May. Chris Goldsmith said he couldn't subpoena me, but he thought it would help Micheal's case if I could go and give evidence as a character witness in the closing stages of the retrial. Could I travel to Houston on 13 June and stay until the fifteenth, as they weren't sure when I would be called?

I said I would consider it very carefully but needed to discuss it with a number of people before making a decision. After talking to Vic and to the chair of the charity I was working for, I decided to go. I had no idea if my evidence would make any difference, but Micheal needed to know that I was prepared to do this for him. It had never occurred to me that we might ever meet, and I worried that he would find me a disappointment.

The chair of the charity I worked for had lived in Texas and told me it would be very hot and humid while I was there. She brought me an armful of lightweight cotton jackets and other suitable clothing for me to borrow.

Faxes were being exchanged daily with Chris Goldsmith, and he told me that Micheal's sister, Pat, wanted me to stay with her and her family rather than go to a hotel. I was very pleased to hear this news but also apprehensive about how we would get on.

I arrived at Houston in the late afternoon, looking for someone from the attorney's office who I was expecting to meet me. A very smartly dressed young woman approached me and asked, 'Are you Lesley?' It was Pat; she had her son, Chad, with her. My case was quickly loaded into the pick-up truck and we were off onto the freeway system to Pat's home. The truck had air conditioning and so it wasn't until we reached her home that I felt the full impact of the heat and the humidity.

Pat had been going to the court for three weeks to attend the retrial and had been taking freshly laundered shirts and other clothes each day for Micheal to wear. Other members of the family had also attended regularly.

I learned a lot from Pat about the dreadful childhoods all five children had endured. Their father had disciplined them with an electric cattle prod and sexually abused all three girls. In 1980, he and Micheal's mother, Louella, were involved in an automobile accident which left him quadraplegic and totally dependent. Louella was also injured in the accident, and in addition to her injuries, she was also coping with diabetes and a heart condition. Micheal's father had died two months before the retrial, and Pat had rallied the family to arrange and attend the funeral.

One thing that had puzzled me was that Micheal had said early in our correspondence that his mother had been murdered; yet Louella was alive. Pat explained that Micheal had left home in his teens to escape his father's abuse. He had lived with an aunt, and after his aunt died, he was helped by an elderly lady who was kind to him, fed him and became his substitute mother. In return he did chores for her. It was this woman who had been murdered.

Pat had been in the United States Army and said she had benefited from the discipline and learned to set goals for herself. She and her husband, Paul, had a number of businesses. The main one is a construction business, building custom-designed homes for people. They had recently bought a 30-acre plot to use as the site for low-cost housing offering a choice of one of five designs to enable people on lower incomes to get a foothold in the housing market. They also had restaurants in Louisiana, where Pat spent three months each year. She had worked as a model, and had training as a beauty therapist to fall back on. She studied continuously, building up skills so that if one was less in demand she had others to use. Her daughter, Tiffany, was training to be a doctor, and Chad, at fifteen, wanted to be an engineer.

Pat had grasped the fact that she could either allow her dreadful childhood to dominate the rest of her life, or she could face it and then put it behind her.

*

In the evening, Pat and I went to meet Chris Goldsmith and his colleagues so that they could tell me what would happen in court.

We met in a crowded restaurant; it was difficult to hear what they were saying. They were lively people and spoke with respect and fondness about Micheal. The work was being done on a *pro bono* basis. The retrial was drawing to an end; my role was not to comment on the facts of the case, but to describe the impression I had gained of Micheal during our five years' correspondence. The district attorney, who was prosecuting, was a young woman. This was her first capital-charge case and she was determined to 'win'. District attorneys are political appointments and they need to win cases to progress in their careers. Apart from the political element, it is the same in the United Kingdom, but I found it sickening that someone should 'progress' by ensuring the death of a fellow human being.

It was hard to take in all the details of the trial procedures. I was very tired after working flat out to ensure that the charity's work continued smoothly while I was away. Then there was the long flight and the anxiety about helping Micheal as much as possible when I gave evidence.

The room that Pat had prepared for me was comfortable, but it was hard to get to sleep. The next morning we left early and went to a restaurant for breakfast on the way to the court. The city was decked out with banners and a whole building was covered with a huge sign saying 'GO ROCKETS!'. Nearly every car had a sticker – the Houston team was in the final of the national basketball championships. They had won in 1994 and there was great excitement at the prospect of another victory.

At the court, Pat took me to meet Betty, Micheal's other sister, and his mother, Louella. Betty's teenage daughter Brandy was there, too, and Chad. The Richards are a very good-looking family and they had all turned out in their best clothes for Micheal.

Pat spoke to one of the court officials and learned that I would probably be called that morning. We waited, feeling tense. Micheal hadn't been told that I was coming in case anything prevented me from travelling. Betty was called to give evidence and was tearful on her return, as was Brandy, who had heard for the first time the full details of her mother's suffering as a child.

Micheal's expression when I walked into the court will stay with me for the rest of my life. As Pat said, 'he just lit up'. The room had a low ceiling, with white walls, and the furniture was made of a light wood. It looked familiar from television series; prosecution and defence lawyers seated at tables facing the judge. The jury was seated to the left-hand side of the judge's bench.

Micheal was sitting with the defence team, not in a dock. He looked smart in a light-blue shirt, well-pressed trousers and patterned tie. His hair was closely cropped and he was much thinner than he had been in the photographs taken in 1991. The stress of waiting for the retrial and the weeks of the retrial itself had taken their toll.

I wanted very much to go over to him, but this wasn't possible. It wasn't even possible to look too much at him, but we did exchange broad smiles.

I was shown to the witness stand. I caused a minor stir when I declined to swear an oath – I am a Quaker, and this doesn't fit with our way of doing things. I was allowed to affirm instead. The judge looked half asleep. I had brought a selection of Micheal's letters and the handkerchiefs he had sent me.

Chris asked me how long I had been writing to Micheal; he also informed the court that my own daughter had been murdered. He asked what impression I had formed of Micheal during our years of correspondence. I responded as best I could and then the district attorney rose to put her questions. She was very aggressive and virtually rubbished everything I had said. People could lie in letters; it wasn't possible to know anything about people by writing to them. I demurred, saying that on the contrary, my experience had been that people often reveal a great of deal of themselves in letters, sometimes more than they would to people they met face to face.

It was all over quickly. After a short break outside the courtroom, we went to sit at the back of the court to hear the rest of the morning's evidence. Pat pointed out that Mr Dixon, the husband of the woman Micheal had killed, was in the court with one of his daughters. The session finished at lunchtime and one of the bailiffs came across to me and said that if I would like to wait, he would give me a few minutes to talk to Micheal before he was taken back to the prison. This was an unexpected opportunity and also a challenge. What could I say to Micheal to support him while he was going through such an ordeal?

In fact, we didn't speak straight away, but just hugged each other. He said he had been amazed to hear my name called as a witness. I asked him how he felt the trial was going for him and if he had any idea what the verdict might be. He said that he was 'hoping for the best but prepared for the worst'. The attorneys hadn't made any predictions. I had my camera with me and the bailiff took some pictures of us together, and I took some of Micheal. All too quickly, he was led away in handcuffs to the prison, the next building along from the courthouse.

Micheal had been deprived of friendly human contact for many years. He hadn't been able to touch his family since he was convicted; the retrial had at least given him the chance to do this. How would he cope if the verdict went against him?

On the way back to Pat's home, we stopped to look for Scott, Micheal's only brother. Pat explained that he had been living rough for years and she tried to keep an eye out for him. We found him, but he had little to say.

We went to a shop and bought T-shirts and baseball caps to wear while we watched the basketball final in the evening. I had asked Micheal if he would be able to see the game, and he said he would be watching it, so although we wouldn't be together, we would share that experience as it was happening.

The rules of basketball and other American games are a bit of a mystery to me, but I was given a crash course before we settled down to watch the game. A lot of tension was released with great whoops of joy as the Rockets pulled ahead and won their second championship.

★

We went back to the court the next morning, expecting the jury to be sent out to consider their verdict. By the appointed time for the start of the day's proceedings, several jury members hadn't arrived. The judge said that he would wait for a few more minutes. I thought that if the missing jury members didn't arrive, the case would have to be adjourned, but this wasn't to be. The judge summed up and sent the jury members present away to consider their verdict.

During the two-hour wait for their return, we sat in the courtroom; more members of Micheal's family had arrived: aunts and uncles and cousins.

When the jury returned, the judge said that before he asked them for their verdict he would state that he wanted no outbursts from people in the courtroom during or after the verdict. He asked jury members for their decision one by one. Each one replied 'guilty' to the charge of first-degree murder.

The courtroom was still and quiet, apart from a yelp of delight from the district attorney. I looked at Louella and at Pat and the rest of the family. They were all looking at Micheal, who was sitting rigidly with his defence team. He was quickly led away and I noticed Mr Dixon go to have a word with him.

I spoke briefly to Mr Dixon's daughter to say how sorry I was about her mother's death. Although I had given evidence for Micheal, I hoped she would realise that I could empathise with her family's situation. She smiled and said that she and her father had come to the retrial to see if any more facts might be revealed about her mother's death. She seemed a very gentle young woman, with a cloud of auburn hair framing her fair-skinned face.

The defence team's demeanour was in marked contrast to the triumph being expressed by the district attorney. They had worked long and hard to prepare Micheal's defence.

Pat gathered everyone together and we walked to the car park to travel home in the pick-up truck and the other family vehicles. Louella started to sway and moan, and gradually a huge sound of shared grief built up. It echoed around the large open space, surging towards the other people in the car park who stood staring as the family expressed their anguish at the verdict. I felt helpless to do anything to assuage their suffering and stood a little to one side, trying to stay calm while taking in the dreadful consequences of the verdict.

Before I left to travel to Texas, I had learned through LifeLines that an unsuccessful retrial often resulted in an execution date being set quickly and carried out, with the appeals being dealt with at top speed. How would Micheal cope with going back to Huntsville after being in the prison in Houston, where the regime was at least a bit more humane?

Louella was so distressed that I began to wonder if she would collapse completely; her breathing was fast and shallow, her eyes rolled upwards. Gradually, her sobs subsided; she was helped gently into the pick-up truck, and we all travelled back to Pat's house.

After a while, the other members of the family left to go to their own homes. It was now late afternoon. Pat suggested that we should go to the prison in the evening to see Micheal. It was impossible to know how he was feeling.

In the sultry early evening, we went along the now familiar route of the half-hour journey from the suburbs to the centre of Houston. Flags waved everywhere, rejoicing at the success of the Rockets; the victory parade would be held the next morning, but we had nothing to celebrate.

Pat had been to the prison many times and knew some of the prison staff. She explained that I was in Houston on a very short visit from England and asked if it would be possible for both of us to see Micheal. After some consultation, this was agreed, and we waited to find out if Micheal would want to see us.

The visiting room was a great shock. Most of the space was taken up with a central area enclosed with toughened glass and metal. At intervals there were small metal mesh inserts, like tea strainers, with the dome facing outwards. Micheal came in wearing horrible shabby orange pyjamas. His brief period of wearing ordinary clothes was over. At first, there weren't many other visitors, so by bending down to speak through the 'tea strainer' and then turning your head so that your ear was against it, you could have a conversation of sorts. Micheal said that after returning from the court he had gone onto the roof of the prison for a game of handball and then returned to his cell to sleep.

He was making a great effort to be cheerful, and he and Pat exchanged banter, talking about the Rockets' win and speculating as to whether Micheal would be able to hear the parade which would go near the prison the next morning.

I felt very inhibited; I didn't know what to say, and as more people arrived I found it difficult to hear anything. Soon the staff signalled that our time was up. We put our hands palm to palm either side of the glass and said goodbye.

*

Pat and I went to eat at a restaurant on the way home. She said that people would be curious as to why we were eating together, as it was still unusual in the American South to see black and white people socialising together.

The flight home was the next afternoon. Pat asked if I would like to go into Houston and see some of the sights in the morning. She said she thought she knew somewhere that I would enjoy seeing. We walked through some botanical gardens with subtropical plants and then went to the Houston Children's Museum. The only other time I had been to America was on a work trip to see children's museums in 1980. It was a treat; we both enjoyed seeing the visiting children's excitement and I was able to buy some small gifts to take home for the family.

Pat took me to the airport and waited with me until I could go through to the departure lounge for my flight. She bore a great deal of responsibility within the family and for the business, for which there had been little time during the weeks of the retrial.

My journey back was sleepless, partly because the plane

was crowded and smoky and partly because of all the thoughts that were whirling around in my head. I was so happy to see Vic, who had come to meet me.

Chapter Seventeen
The meeting

JUST AFTER MY RETURN from Texas, a letter arrived from Jim Fotheringham, Andrew Steel's home probation officer:

> I can understand how the meeting between the three of us in Leicester will have seemed like a repetition of the earlier one. I have since spoken to Eric. The value of it for him was in confirming how you hoped a meeting with Andrew Steel would proceed, and whether there had been any changes of emphasis or intention in the months that had ensued since December. It was important also in terms of how he will tackle the most difficult part of all: making the formal approaches to the management team at Gartree for permission to hold a visit in the admin block.
>
> Andrew Steel has been trying to write you a letter. He is not applying himself very effectively to that at the moment because there has been a lot of resettling to do since he came back from Maidstone. He has indicated to Eric that August would be his choice of month for a visit to take place. I have asked that something definite be proposed, so that you can know where you stand.
>
> If nothing has happened a week from now, I shall call Eric again. I am as sorry as you are that it is taking so long, and am hoping the end result will have been worth it for yours and Andy's sakes.

I replied saying that August would be a good month for me. I contacted Roma and we compared diaries and identified three days when we were both free and sent them to Jim. By mid-July, no date had been suggested, and both Roma and I had to make other arrangements for that week and needed to know the date of the meeting. I contacted Jim several times, but by 1 August still no date had been set.

In the middle of August, I had a telephone call from Jim. It wasn't to confirm that the meeting had been arranged but to say that the prison governor had decided to check with the Home Office before agreeing to it going ahead. The decision was now at a 'very high' Civil Service level and might need to go to a minister for a final decision.

I was very upset and oscillating between tears and rage at this news. It was by now nearly a year since I went to YTV and the first contact was made formally to request a meeting through the channel provided by the Victims' Charter. Jim took the brunt of my frustration. 'I could write for a visitor's order now that I know that Andrew Steel is willing to meet me,' I said. 'Yes, you could, but that would not be the best way for you or for him,' replied Jim. He went on to say that the Home Office had promised a 'quick response'.

This further delay left me feeling very depressed, and although I could see that the governor would feel the need to protect himself, I couldn't accept that it had taken so long for a decision to be made. After all, months had gone by and one meeting already been cancelled, so he must have been aware of my request for some time. No one, apart from Jim and Eric, seemed to consider my needs and feelings in all this. August was the best time for the meeting to happen for me, as I would have time to prepare for and absorb the outcome of the meeting, as my workload would be lighter.

I wrote to Andrew Steel, realising that the cancellation must have had an impact on him, too, and fearful that the further delay might mean that he would reconsider his decision and withdraw. In my letter I said:

It now seems very unlikely that we will be able to meet next week
because further arrangements need to be agreed by the prison. I hope

that despite this setback you will still be willing to go ahead with the
meeting and that it won't be too long now.

September came with no response from the Home Office, and on the eighth I wrote to Jim to let him know that I was going to be away from 18 to 27 September. The letter continued:

My autumn workload is going to be incredibly heavy. From the week I
get back from holiday we have an event in every week, plus many other
meetings and some major projects to complete or start, quite apart from
the day to day work. I am hoping to arrange to be on leave from the 18th
December — 2nd January and the week beginning 11th December is and
should remain reasonably clear. What I am saying is that I don't think
I can, in time or other terms, cope with a meeting with Andrew Steel
until mid-December. I did write to him briefly after the meeting in
August fell through, and hope that he will understand that it isn't
because I want to cause him any problems that I don't want to arrange
anything in next two and a half months.

Roma and I sent the dates in December on which we were both free to Jim.

Jim contacted me in October to say there was still no response from the Home Office. I noted dryly that no one from the Home Office had contacted me. Throughout that busy period of work it was at the back of my mind that maybe the decision wouldn't come through in time and the process was going to be prolonged even further. But I wasn't going to give up.

No news came in October or November. On 1 December, I wrote to Jim.

Sorry to be nagging you again but it would be very helpful to have some
information as to whether the meeting at Gartree will be going ahead

later this month, and if so, which date or dates are possible.

As I'm sure you'll appreciate I need to let Roma know as soon as possible now and I'm also wanting to do other things in the lead up to Christmas and can't make arrangements until the Gartree date is known.

On the same day, the principal psychologist was writing to me, but his letter did not reach me until 7 December.

The purpose of this letter is to invite you to a mediation meeting with Andrew Steel, to introduce myself and to outline the proposed arrangements for the mediation meeting.

I am the Principal Psychologist who has responsibility for the Management of the Gartree Therapeutic Community (GTC) in which Andrew Steel is a resident. As the manager of the GTC I have been closely involved in the process of negotiating with the Prison Service the mechanisms required to enable the meeting to take place. I have also been responsible for the preparation of Andrew Steel in terms of his therapy within the community.

My understanding is that you have suggested several dates on which you would be available to come to such a meeting. I would like to suggest that Monday the 11th December is the most suitable day.

I have suggested that no more than four people should be involved in the actual meeting, yourself and companion, Andrew Steel and either myself or Mr Scott. You have already met Mr Scott, he is the probation officer attached to the Gartree Therapeutic Community. We are arranging a meeting place that is away from the normal visiting area in order to ensure a suitable environment for such a meeting to take place. I am conscious that you will be travelling to and from the meeting and would therefore like to suggest that the meeting take place at 2 o'clock p.m. and be scheduled to end at half past three. This will provide time for yourself to spend time with your companion before the need to travel. I also think it wise that a time boundary be placed on the meeting in order for everyone to know what the boundaries are. The fact that this amount of time is set aside does of course not mean that it needs to be used or that either you or Andrew Steel cannot initiate a break in the meeting if either of you feel this would be helpful.

Please contact me, either at the above number or by letter to let me know if the above is acceptable or whether you want to discuss arrangements further. I am conscious of the fact that this meeting is of great importance to both yourself and Andrew Steel and want to facilitate you both to the best of our ability. I look forward to hearing from you.

I reread this letter several times and was struck by the odd conjunction of formality, even pomposity, and the wish to be helpful. It felt as if the psychologist had had great difficulty in writing the letter. I wanted the fourth person at the meeting to be Eric, rather than someone I hadn't met before.

The date was for the week I had suggested, but the notice was very short. I phoned Roma at home early in the morning and was relieved to hear that she could still take time off work to come with me.

Later that morning, I phoned the prison to confirm that Roma and I would travel to the prison, and arrangements were made for the principal psychologist, Roland, to meet us from the station.

When Vic came home from work that evening, I let him know that the date had at long last been confirmed.

I was very tense over the weekend. I kept looking at the questions I had prepared some months before. I didn't want the meeting to be like an interrogation, and yet I wanted answers. It was impossible to know how it would go, but I was determined to do everything I could to stay calm during the meeting.

★

Monday 11 December. It was a wintry, dark dawn. I was up very early, checking and rechecking the contents of the small briefcase I would be taking with me. Roma and I had agreed to take a packed lunch to eat on the train. I packed knitting, not knowing if I would be able to hold the needles securely.

I travelled into London far sooner than I needed, not wanting a train cancellation or delay to make me late in arriving at St Pancras. Everything ran on time; I had an hour and a half to wait before it was time to meet Roma. On impulse, I decided to go to John Lewis in Oxford Street; when I got there, I found that the shop would be open half an hour later than usual because of staff training. I paced around the four sides of the closed building, looking at the window displays. Once inside, I looked around the fabric department. In the remnant boxes there were some lovely pieces of material. I stroked the velvets and started turning over the pile. I thought I would make some dolls' clothes for my grand-daughter, Marianne, with some of the pretty fabrics. I bought several small pieces, then wondered why I had done so as my sewing competence is very limited and projects usually end in disappointment. The bag of fabric would not fit into the brief-case, so I now had two bags to carry.

Back on the Victoria line to King's Cross, then to St Pancras station to wait for Roma. I was still half an hour early. I sat on one of the benches to wait. Out of the corner of my eye I could see a young man moving from person to person and assumed he was asking for change. He approached, and stand-ing directly in front of me he thrust the insides of his wrists, which were bleeding, out of his coat so that they were within a few inches of my face and said, 'Help me, help me, I've been stabbed, can you give me some money?'

This was one of the few parts of Ruth's body that had not

been stabbed. Why did this have to happen to me on this day when I needed to preserve all my self-control? The wounds were superficial and probably self-inflicted. There was a British Rail staff member nearby, and I called him over and asked for the young man to be taken to the first-aid room for attention. I was still shaking when Roma arrived a few minutes later.

⋆

On the train, I did knit for part of the journey, finding the repetitive movements and touch of the smooth, soft yarn soothing.

I suggested two conditions that I thought might be presented to us on arrival, though nothing had been said in advance. The first was that we might have to be searched. I thought that would be a reasonable request, as I might have put up a credible front and yet plan to attack Andrew Steel during the meeting and be carrying a concealed weapon. The second was that I might be asked to give an undertaking that I would not speak or write about the meeting. I wasn't prepared to give such an undertaking; I would rather turn back without the meeting going ahead.

The train was on time. We were the only two passengers to get off at Market Harborough. The station was deserted and desolate in the windless, murky day. A long flight of stairs descended from the platform to the dark tunnel leading to the booking office and exit.

There was only one person in the exit area. We introduced ourselves to Roland, the principal psychologist, and went outside to get in the car. One of the first pieces of information we were given was that Eric would be present at the meeting, not Roland, at Andrew Steel's request. Without wanting to hurt Roland's feelings by expressing my pleasure at this news,

I did comment that I thought it would be helpful to have someone who knew both Andrew Steel and myself to facilitate the meeting.

Roland was at pains to point out how many people had been involved in making the arrangements, and the problems of finding an appropriate place for the meeting to be held. It wasn't possible to let me too far into the prison or Andrew Steel too far out of the secure areas.

He was proud of the fact that they had now established a protocol in case any future requests were made. I was both irritated and pleased at hearing this news. I didn't want to be distracted with the problems of the prison staff at this time, yet I was pleased that if anyone approached the prison in future, their path should be easier than mine had been.

It wasn't far from the station to the prison. The bleak, flat fields of the East Midlands passed by until we turned into a road called Gallow Field Lane. What a location for a prison where offenders convicted of the most serious crimes were serving their sentences!

High wire fences surrounded a sprawl of low buildings. The entry gate was opened and we drove through part of the grounds. We were taken to a side door of one of the buildings. Click, click went the locks before the prison officer inside opened the door. Was this where we might be searched? No, we were told that a special privilege had been granted. We, the green-and-white John Lewis bag containing the fabrics and our briefcases were not searched.

We were taken upstairs and at the top there was Eric. We hugged and I said how pleased I was that he would be facilitating the meeting.

The meeting was to be held in the boardroom. It was a grim place; dark wood-effect plastic covered the walls. It was almost filled by a heavy wooden central table surrounded by wooden upright chairs.

In the little space left at the side of the room was a small, square coffee table with an armless easychair on each side. On the table was a cyclamen in bloom, bearing fuchsia-pink flowers above its patterned foliage. I glanced back at the door; the glass insert had been taped over. It was 1.40 p.m. – twenty minutes before the meeting was due to start.

The four of us sat down and Eric went over the arrangements.

I had already asked if Roma could take notes during the meeting so that I didn't have to try to remember everything as well as think. Eric said he would check again when Andrew Steel arrived and ask him to confirm that he had no objections.

Then Roland left to fetch Andrew Steel from his wing. Eric turned to me and said fiercely, 'This meeting is for *you*. *You* must get what *you* want from it. Don't think about Andrew Steel's needs. That's our job and we will be here for him afterwards.'

Roma got her notebook out and the three of us sat for a few minutes, eyes fixed on the closed door. My heart was thumping and I wondered if Eric and Roma were also feeling a rush of adrenalin. After all this time, would this meeting achieve what I wanted or would I go away feeling crushed and disappointed?

I heard approaching footsteps. The door opened and the frame seemed to be filled with a stocky man, dressed in sports gear, his hair in dreadlocks pulled back from his face. He was breathing heavily and perspiration beaded his brow.

Roland peered around Andrew Steel's shoulder and said he would be in his office if he was needed, then closed the door. Andrew Steel walked into the room and sat down on the chair facing me.

He didn't look up as Eric went over the arrangements for the meeting and nodded to confirm that he had no objections to Roma taking notes.

There was a long pause and then Andrew Steel said, 'I'm lost for words. Someone help please.'

I asked him if we had ever met at Ruth's house and he said we had never met before. I asked him how he had got to know Ruth — I thought this would be an easy question for him to answer as he had already written to tell me about this. He began,

'Tom invited me to the house. The first time not much was said. At Ruth's birthday party I met other girls and started going out with one of them. Then various times Tom called me and I visited the house. We listened to music, having a laugh. Ruth joined in.

'It is difficult for me to say certain things. Lots of understanding I have to do for myself — what was happening at the time. In a situation I couldn't understand for myself. Ruth was the only person I could talk to — she helped me a lot. Hardest part was that I couldn't give that help back.'

I said it was hard for me to understand why he killed her when he said that she had helped him. I asked if he had known that Ruth was on her own in the house that night. He replied,

'Shall I tell you what was going on? Tom was cheating on Ruth. He put me between him and Claire, Libby and Ruth. I had to lie to her and cover for Tom every time. Ruth was suspecting something, but I couldn't say anything. Deep down Ruth never believed me. He was with Claire a lot of that time. I was seeing Libby. I had just broken up with my missus and little kid, dealing with that, grandfather died. Everything in front of me falling apart, I had no control over it. No control in my mind.'

I wanted him to get on with explaining what had happened so I asked him to confirm that he had been at Claire's flat and then gone to Finsbury Park and then to Ruth's house in Enfield. He hesitated and then launched into what sounded like something he had rehearsed in advance of the meeting.

'That day I'd been taking drugs all day and drinking alcohol. At 9 p.m. I took more drugs – LSD. I phoned Tom, they were going out – him, Claire and Libby and asked me to bring LSD back. Because of the state of my mind I lost all track of time and got to Claire's at 10.30 to 11 p.m. It was too late to go out and everyone was in a bad mood with me. In my state of mind I shoved it all off. There was drink left from a party and I had more. I had to go somewhere that night but no one was there. With all the tension I went to Ruth feeling down and confused. I turned to Ruth for help. Do you want me to go on?'

I nodded quickly, my heart beating fast and mind fully concentrated; I didn't want him to stop when I was about to hear his version of what had happened at the house.

'I got on a bus to Enfield, walked to Ruth's house, knocked and Ruth answered. Went into the kitchen, talking. Ruth kept asking where Tom was, I found myself stuck – couldn't get out with all the stuff going on, I started to get lost inside it all. An argument broke out – "Tell me where Tom is." "Please, I can't." I didn't want her to question me. Ruth started to get upset. I only reached out to say calm down. With the way I was I must have looked bad to Ruth. Tom and I decided not tell Ruth about trips etc. She wouldn't know what condition I was in. I reached out; my eyes must have been glittering. Ruth hit me hard said "Get away." Ruth ran off shouting; from there I totally lost control. I've never really seen that. I tried to explore it in my group, my gut feeling said no. I've never been able to see it yet I remember being on the stairs with the bag in my hand that I threw away. Got back to Tom somehow. I got frightened, couldn't picture what it was. Didn't go to grandfather's funeral. Woke up. Tom said "Let's go." Something said don't go back to the house but I went. Little cats jumped out and I saw Ruth. That frightened me.'

There was a silence while I tried to take in what he had said. He'd knocked at the door and Ruth had let him in. He hadn't used a key or entered at the back through an unlocked door. As far as I knew, the relationship with Tom had finished just after Christmas and had been in trouble for a long time before then, so this account of Ruth wanting to know where he was may have been about the money he owed her, but I would never know. Despite the drugs and alcohol Andrew Steel had taken, he was alert enough to travel back to Palmers Green and also to remember the next day that he didn't want to go to the house. How frightened Ruth must have been – yet she had tried to defend herself. Why didn't she run out of the front door instead of going upstairs? Who knows what people do when confronted by 'glittering eyes'? The fact that Tom and he had concealed their drug-taking was also odd – did he mean that Ruth didn't take drugs?

I asked if he was saying that Ruth had never taken drugs. He said quickly:

'Ruth wasn't a drug taker, not at all, the only thing, now and again, cannabis, not regular, one-offs. Social things because of the way Tom and I were. Ruth liked Bacardi. She was a very nice friend.'

I knew she liked Bacardi. We used to tease her and say she

would grow out of it because she drank it with blackcurrant that looked like cough mixture to us. I hadn't known that she had taken cannabis but wasn't unduly shocked, knowing how common it was among her generation.

I then asked if he wanted to know what had happened to our family on the second of February. He nodded. I told him that I had been away on a work trip until Wednesday 31 January, and when I got home there was a message from Ruth saying she wanted to talk about something and had hoped I would be at home so that she could come and see me; she would contact me again on Thursday. I phoned her but she was out and so the last time I heard her voice was the recorded message on her answerphone. On Friday 2 February, I went to see a friend who was in hospital following an operation for cancer. The police came to our door just as we were finishing our evening meal. They didn't tell us how she died but said she had been found in suspicious circumstances. We had gone to see Catherine and my mother. I had known that the break-up with Tom had happened and that Ruth was waiting for him to find somewhere else to live.

Andrew Steel reacted quickly, saying, 'That's news to me – that Tom was planning to move out of the house.'

I said that we had known that Tom's behaviour to Ruth hadn't been good, but we had felt that we shouldn't interfere and had been relieved when the relationship had finished of its own accord. She had met someone new early in January.

He said, 'Yes, I knew that, but I thought Ruth was trying to get back at Tom. I never knew she wanted him out of the house. I thought they had an argument and both wanted some space.'

That hadn't been my impression at all, as Ruth had wanted to finish the relationship for a long time. I think he was right in saying that she knew Tom had been seeing other women while still living in the house and claiming to be her partner.

I told Andrew Steel that she had been to see us during the week before she died and had said she might want to come back to live with us for a while as things were difficult for her. I remembered thinking very carefully before responding to her, as I didn't want her to feel that she had failed in any way, and wanted to leave the decision to her.

I went on:

'On Saturday the third of February, Geoff Parratt came to see us and said that you and Tom were in custody. It was the first time I had heard your name. It was very confusing, as this was the first time we were aware that somebody had killed her. Then we went to see Vic's side of the family. It was awful having to tell so many people that Ruth was dead. There were over two hundred people at her funeral, despite the short notice and the postal strike that was on at the time. Her employers held a celebration of her life and had to hire a theatre at Palmers Green to accommodate the number of people who wanted to come. Catherine now has two children who will never know their Auntie Ruth.'

During this account Andrew Steel didn't look at me; his head was lowered, his shoulders were turned inwards. There was a long silence. We had been talking for half an hour.

*

Eric said quietly, 'Would anyone like to have a short break now?' I thought this was a very tactful way of intervening; it didn't put the onus on either of us. Andrew Steel almost whispered, 'Yes.'

Eric used the phone in the room to speak to Roland, who

came to the door and took Roma and I to his office. The corridor was grim, with flimsy boards painted in dull colours dividing the space into uniform boxes. Roland explained that he had a kettle in his room and could make us some tea there. There were no tea-making facilities where staff could meet. The kettle boiled, and Roma and I sat half smiling at each other, wanting to check out how we were feeling and discuss how the meeting had gone so far. I was anxious that we might find Andrew Steel didn't want to continue. Had I gone too far in telling him about the impact of Ruth's death on us? I didn't regret saying any of it, and I had more to say.

*

The phone rang in Roland's office; we returned to the room. Andrew Steel was standing by the window with his back to us. When he turned round, I thought he looked as if he had been crying, but he had now composed himself.

We sat down again. He sucked in a deep breath and, looking directly at me, launched himself into speech.

'I find it hard to look at you. Not only for the pain I've given you and your family. I'm not seeing you. I'm seeing Ruth and I'm finding that very hard. Before I came over for the visit, I used to say to the group, it won't only be Lesley Moreland to see but Ruth. I can actually see Ruth. I find it very hard.'

I recognised that he wasn't talking about physical resemblance, though in our family Ruth was generally thought to look more like me and Catherine more like Vic. I felt that he had been made to confront what he had done in a tangible way for the first time. But his repetition of it being hard for him also indicated that he was still very absorbed in his own feelings.

I asked him what he thought about the trial and the cancellation of the first date.

'I've never been asked that question. I've always said to myself I should have got more. Judge said fourteen years, Chief Justice twelve. Gave me ten, plus three.'

This was the first time I had heard the details of the judge's recommendation. I hadn't known that the Lord Chief Justice had been involved.

Eric explained that Andrew Steel had ten years to serve as the punishment part of his sentence, and this would then be reviewed by the parole board; he could then be moved to a less secure prison. This decision would be based on how he had behaved during the ten years. If all went well for him, he would be released on licence at the end of thirteen years and would be closely supervised for four years after release. At the end of four years, supervision would be discontinued, but he would be on licence for the rest of his life.

I asked how he had felt about having to be moved from Wormwood Scrubs because my friend Jane worked there.

'When I was in reception, the governor said I couldn't stay. There was a lot of confusion at that time. When I first met Jane, I kept myself at a distance. I was very scared. She read your message out. I read it to the group. About improving myself – I find it hard to say – I have took them words that you said and will always remember them and I will try to make myself a better person than I was.'

There was no doubt that this message had made an impact on him.

I said that I had wondered if he would receive any help to understand why he had done what he had done, and that my hope was still that when he left prison he would be able to lead a constructive life. I didn't think that was a soft option: to say, 'Work hard and come out as a better person' is a tough task. I was very pleased that he had joined the therapeutic community.

While I was saying this, I glanced at my watch. Time was passing quickly and I hadn't told him all that I wanted to about the impact of his actions. I didn't pause but went on:

'I was surprised at how angry I felt. I wasn't able to work. For the first time in many years I had to ask my husband for money – I really resented this, I had to use all my savings. Not only had this awful thing happened to us but I was having to worry about money.

'Vic went back to work a few weeks after Ruth died. He finds it very difficult; he and Ruth had problems during her adolescence but these had long been resolved and they were very close at the time she died.

'In terms of statutory provision, so much has been pumped into you and nothing for us, except the kindness of individuals involved, like Matt Miller. He sold Ruth's car for us and on the first anniversary of her death he brought us flowers. He was upset when he saw the video of her at work. He felt that he knew her after interviewing so many people. Ruth had already achieved a great deal in her life and had the potential for so much more. I miss her terribly; I still do. We didn't have a perfect relationship, but it was close. We were interested in each other's work. We were doing some craft workshops together and one should have been held the week after she died.

'It would have been her birthday on the sixth of February – my mother-in-law's present to her is still in our loft, unopened. I don't know what to do with it and can't talk to my mother-in-law about it. For the first two years, I felt out of control in public, never knowing if I would start to cry. I never knew I could cry so much.'

He looked stunned. The afternoon sun had moved round and was in his eyes. Roma suggested that he move his chair and he did. This gave him a little time to think before responding.

'I don't know if sorry is the right word. I don't know how to say sorry.'

There was another long silence. He wasn't going to expand on this without prompting. But he had very nearly said he was sorry.

I could have offered him some encouragement, but I had more to say and time was moving on towards the end of the meeting.

'In the autumn before Ruth died, we trimmed an over-grown hedge and hadn't cut it into small enough pieces to take to the dump. By the autumn of 1990, the wood was very hard. Every time I got out the long-armed secateurs to cut it up I thought about you. I was really angry and it was my way of venting it. Our family hasn't fallen apart, our life goes on and brings with it new problems as well as good things.'

He was struggling again, but he looked as if he wanted to say more.

'My mum said that she will never forgive me for what I done to Ruth. She finds it hard to come and see me some-times.'

What was he looking for? Sympathy from me? I said that I had often thought about his family and hoped that in time his mother would come to see that what he had done was one part of him, but he was still her son.

'Can I say something? My expression is not showing tears outside. It is inside. I cry every night. Ruth did mean a lot to me, she was a very close friend. I will never forgive myself. I still read the letters your mother, Joy, sent me. Sometimes I sit there and look at Ruth's photo, from the articles in the papers, and I try to take myself back into what happened. I try every way I can so one day I can actually talk about it. The pain I caused you and your family I regret. I do feel ashamed of myself for what I've done. I am. Sorry.'

He could 'never forgive himself', and his mother had said that she will 'never forgive him'. Could I forgive him? No, I couldn't, and I didn't say anything except to acknowledge that I could see that he was sorry. But what was the sorrow about? It seemed to be more centred on feeling sorry for himself. He cried every night. 'You and me both, sunshine,' I thought.

He must have sensed that I was finding it hard to accept his apology, because he said, 'I hope that one day you do believe me.' It wasn't that I didn't believe him; I did believe that he was sorry he had killed Ruth and he was sorry for the impact on her family and friends. What was his concept of forgiveness? I didn't feel we had a common understanding; it would take time to establish and time was running out. I sat, stony-faced, struggling to find something not too harsh to say and yet speak with honesty, so I said, 'I do appreciate this meeting and that you are saying as much as you can.'

He said that he wished he could support my family and me. This comment prompted me to say that I wanted him to know that I didn't think my mother's letter to him was appropriate and nobody should speak on Ruth's behalf about what had happened.

It was time to turn to the future. I didn't feel there was anything more to be gained by continuing to go over the past.

He said, 'My family are moving out of London. I'll go back and live with my family until I'm ready to start afresh. I'm going to get out to be someone responsible. Make a new start to my life.'

I asked if he heard from Tom. He said he had never written to Tom but had heard that he was still with Claire.

*

Eric said, 'There are eight minutes left. Is there anything either of you want to say or ask?'

'Yes,' Andrew Steel said. 'This has been on my mind since the Scrubs. Jane came to see me and asked about the chain necklace. I haven't got a clue. It's always been on my mind. I've never brought it up. I don't know what happened to it.'

I explained that Catherine had given the necklace to Ruth for her twenty-first birthday, and that before I contacted Jane with the questions I wanted her to ask him, I'd asked Catherine if there was anything she wanted to know. She had asked about the necklace. We never found it, and it upset me that Catherine couldn't have it. We had had only a short time to clear Ruth's things from the house and we didn't find it there, and it wasn't among the possessions that the police returned to us after the trial.

Eric said, 'Sometimes after a meeting people think of something else they wish they had raised.' I said that if that happened, Andrew Steel could write to me care of Jim as before. I didn't want to give him our address.

The minutes were slipping away. We looked at each other and he said, 'The last day at the trial when the verdict came up, I turned around, it was you behind me, wasn't it? When I stopped on the stairs, I wanted to say sorry but I couldn't get the words out. Seeing you now … it's hard to explain, being able to say sorry, not appropriate, but I wanted to do that. I do mean it.'

I hadn't remembered him turning towards us at the end of the trial. I wasn't looking at him as he left the dock, having waved to his family, after the verdict because I wanted to respect his privacy.

I said that I thought it had been helpful for us to meet. 'People have asked me what I thought about you and I had to say that I didn't know because I didn't know you. I have a better idea now.'

⋆

Eric asked Andrew Steel how he was feeling.

'Scared, ashamed, there is no ending. I'm glad you came. What pushed me more was to understand your feelings, what happened to you and your family. I've got to be able to understand that and never let anyone else go through that.'

The time was up. Since Eric had given the 'eight minutes left' signal, I had been thinking about how the meeting would come to an end. I wanted to let Andrew Steel know that I recognised and respected his courage in going through with the meeting and that I did feel he had done his best to give me an account of what had happened. I couldn't say I forgave him. Could I bring myself to shake his hand? If I offered to do so, he would extend his dominant hand, the hand that had taken Ruth's life.

Eric phoned to ask Roland to come to take Andrew Steel back to his wing. All four of us stood up. I said, 'Thank you for coming,' and offered my hand. He took it and we shook hands before he turned and left the room with Roland.

⋆

Eric, Roma and I talked for a few minutes, the tension that had been present throughout the meeting gradually receding.

Roland was going to take us back to the station when he returned from the wing.

On the train back to London, I felt drained and exhausted, not sure yet what the overall effect of the meeting had been. I did feel relieved. Relieved that at long last the meeting had taken place. Relieved that I had achieved the objective of meeting Andrew Steel and would now be able to see him as a person, rather than as a cardboard-cutout character identified only as a murderer. Relieved that he had been able to talk and that he had given an account of what had happened which tallied with the information I already had. He hadn't resorted to lying; I felt that he had done his best to give me the information I needed. He had said that he was sorry, and I hadn't made that one of my expectations, so that was a bonus. I was also relieved that the meeting had used all the time allowed and that I had not wasted time by getting upset or angry. And yet I hadn't been able to forgive him.

There was also a sense of achievement that despite the many obstacles, I had got through the 'system' and achieved what I wanted. It had happened in a way which meant that if anyone else wanted to arrange a similar meeting in that prison, it should be easier for them and for the prison staff and offenders.

Roma tore the pages out of her notebook and gave them to me. I said I would type them up and send them to her for checking.

I got home before Vic. I took the messages off the answerphones, ours and the charity's. It was difficult to engage with requests for booking forms for events and queries about membership. Then I went downstairs to prepare our evening meal.

On Thursday, I phoned Eric. I was curious to find out what

he had thought of the meeting. During our discussion, he said that Andrew Steel had told him that he had had his first night of undisturbed sleep since he had killed Ruth. He also said that Andrew Steel had been afraid that I would hit him. I was very surprised to hear this. 'That would have been impossible,' I said. 'You were between us.' Eric replied, 'What makes you think I would have stopped you?'

*

On the Friday after the meeting, Vic and I went for our weekly session at the local leisure centre to use the sauna, steam room and jacuzzi. We were the only people there. We sat at opposite ends of the steam room, invisible to each other. I asked, 'Do you want to know anything about the visit?'

'No,' he replied.

Chapter Eighteen

Publicity about the meeting

BACK AT WORK, early in 1996, I was approached by The Media Trust. They were trying to find someone who could talk to Internet service providers and identify the key points for charities to consider when selecting one. The proposal was that I would be filmed wearing a Superman outfit and, as 'Supergeek', interviewing four companies who already had charities as clients. This sounded like a fun way to start a new year, but I hoped it wouldn't be necessary to jump off any high buildings!

The day of the filming was a long one. I arrived at The Media Trust's offices just after 7 a.m.; it was late in the evening before the interviews were completed. We returned to the offices for a quick break in the early evening, before filming the final sequences. The director of The Media Trust was still at work. She had heard about Ruth's death, and passed me an invitation she had received to a meeting that the National Association for the Care and Resettlement of Offenders (NACRO) were holding the following week. Correspondents from the broadsheet newspapers and makers of factual radio and television programmes about serious crime had been invited to hear presentations and debate the topic 'Crime and the Media'.

I went to the NACRO meeting intending to listen, with no thought of saying anything. The meeting started with brief presentations from a chief constable, a BBC crime programme producer and Duncan Campbell of the *Guardian*. Each presentation was focused on how the media presents violent crime to its readers or viewers, and the effect this has on the public perception of crime.

When the meeting was opened for questions and comments, it soon got bogged down in an exchange of interpretations of statistical information. The initial presentations raised a number of far more interesting issues, and I put up my hand to indicate that I would like to say something.

I decided to raise four concerns:

—The way that victims of violent crime are portrayed in the media as people whose lives have fallen apart and will have no further meaning. While this may be their initial reaction, it is not the full reality for most people in the longer term. This image provides no alternative role models for future victims of violent crime.

—The growing polarisation – 'bad people are in prison: good people are outside' – enables a false separation to take place and allows people to deny the 'bad' parts of themselves. Since the majority of people in prison are there for non-violent crimes, only a small percentage might really present a physical danger to other people if they were in the community. This also reflects the way in which an individual becomes identified with a single action rather than being seen as a complex human being formed through many experiences and with the capacity to change.

—The lack of information about ways of enabling offenders and victims to pursue alternative options to the adversarial manner in which our criminal justice system works makes it hard to achieve contact even if both parties want it.

—Victims are denied the information and support that might help them to understand what has happened.

I revealed that I had met the man who murdered my daughter in the prison where he was held.

At the end of the meeting, Duncan Campbell rushed up the aisle. I thought he was in a hurry to leave, but he approached me and asked if he could have a few minutes to talk to me. The man sitting next to me said he would like to join in – he was Stuart Tendler, senior crime correspondent for *The Times*.

They both wanted to interview me, and offered to see me together so that I wouldn't have to go over the same ground twice. We met at a hotel near King's Cross two weeks later and talked for over two hours. They were both good company, and it was my first opportunity to hear the reactions of people who had not been involved in the preparations for my meeting with Andrew Steel. They had heard of no one else who had wanted to meet the person who had murdered a member of their family and who had achieved this by approaching staff at a prison. I was still thinking about the outcomes of the meeting; I recognised it would take a long while for all its repercussions to be absorbed. Talking to the journalists, I realised that I had achieved much of what I had set out to do. Andrew Steel would now serve his sentence with some understanding of what he had done; hopefully this would make him less likely to be violent in the future. I could now see him as a person, though not someone I could say I liked. I still didn't understand why he had killed Ruth, but he had tried to answer my questions and I had heard his description of what had happened so far as he could remember.

★

Before the journalists' articles were published, we found out that my mother had secondary tumours. She had had a mastectomy following breast cancer nearly sixteen years before and, apart from a minor recurrence that had been dealt with in day surgery, she had been free of cancer since. She hadn't been well since the previous summer, when shingles had left her looking and feeling very frail. We went together to see the oncology consultant. She was told that an operation, radiotherapy or chemotherapy would be impossible at this stage, so treatment would be palliative only. She wasn't told explicitly that she was terminally ill. I wasn't clear whether she understood that she had effectively been told her life was coming to an end. I felt I should wait for her to say something, rather than explore this with her so soon after the news had been broken.

My sorrow for my mother in facing this blow was complicated by my horror at the location of one of the secondary tumours. It was in her neck, in the same position as Ruth's major wound.

*

On 26 February, the *Guardian* and *The Times* published their articles. Both were straightforward accounts of the facts about my meeting with Andrew Steel. Duncan Campbell had phoned me the day before to read his copy to me, so I was prepared for the final paragraph:

> In Lesley's bag is a wallet of photographs of Ruth, taken from one of the training videos she made. The impression is of an outgoing young woman, full of the enjoyment of life, one who would no doubt be proud of how her parents are trying to deal with her death. At the back of the wallet is a blonde lock, as if a question mark as to how anyone could have harmed a hair of her head.

It had never occurred to me that the lock of Ruth's hair is in the shape of a question mark. The blue ribbon that ties it provides the gap between the longer curl and the short straight piece below the bow that forms the dot.

There were over thirty phone calls from television researchers and radio and print journalists on the day the articles appeared, all requesting further interviews. I parried them all, explaining that my mother was seriously ill and in hospital and we were still waiting for a full prognosis. I suggested that they should call back in two weeks, if they were still interested in an interview. This was the genuine situation. However, I was also aware that it would deter those who didn't have a serious interest.

★

I went to see our GP, who said that while it was difficult to predict the course the cancer would take, he didn't expect my mother to live for more than a few months. I decided to resign from my job so that I could have time to be with her for what remained of her life.

Early in May, my mother said that she knew she wasn't going to get better. That enabled us to talk through some of our long-standing misunderstandings and hurts. Over the next three weeks, she gradually grew weaker, then she said, 'I've had enough, I want to go soon.'

The last time I saw her fully conscious, the day before she died at the end of May, we parted with laughter. She took a daily paper that featured a competition offering cash prizes. We had been checking her numbers each day during my lunchtime visit. We thought she had a winning combination, then realised that we had been looking at the wrong numbers for that day.

I spent my birthday planning her funeral. My mother had

said she had no particular wishes, but we felt that it was right to return to the crematorium near Watford where my father's and Ruth's ashes were scattered near each other in the beautiful grounds.

It was hard to go back there. Catherine said she felt as if her grandmother had been cheated, because all of us were thinking so much about Ruth at her funeral.

Chapter Nineteen
An attempt to meet a member of
Andrew Steel's family

TOWARDS THE END of November 1996, I was contacted by an organisation called the Centre for Crime and Justice Studies. I knew some of their staff, as the organisation had been members of the charity I had worked for. Their director had given an excellent presentation on charity newsletters at one of the seminars we organised. The Centre's work brings together both professionals and laypeople who are interested in the criminal justice system.

They, together with Mediation UK, were planning to hold a conference 'Repairing the Damage – Restorative Justice in Action' at Bristol University in March 1997, and the director asked me if I would be willing to talk about my meeting with Andrew Steel. The audience would include prison-service staff, probation officers, police officers, Victim Support scheme co-ordinators, mediators and civil servants. The other presenters were drawn from a wide range of work, and included Dr Mark Umbreit, one of the leading American academics specialising in restorative justice.

Restorative justice was a new phrase to me. I found a book by Martin Wright (who had made contact with the prison chaplain for me in 1991) entitled *Justice for Victims and Offenders – A Restorative Response to Crime*. He defined restorative justice as 'a form of criminal justice based on reparation'. Reparation constituted 'actions to repair the damage caused by crime, either materially (at least in part) or symbolically. Usually performed by the offender, in the form of payment or service to the victim, if there is one and the victim wishes it, or to the community, but can include the offender's co-operation in training, counselling or therapy.'

Our current retributive justice system, based on punishment, operates in a way that keeps the people most directly involved in a crime apart. I had discovered for myself how hard it was to establish any contact, and I hoped to find ways to help other people who might want to follow a similar path to my own. I agreed to speak at the conference to provide a real-life experience from a family member of a victim of crime.

*

The anniversary of Ruth's death was looming again. Having thought I was getting the hang of coping with early February, I was taken by surprise and suddenly felt really low and miserable. My distress centred around the loss of her future. What would she have been doing with her life at the age of thirty-one? I couldn't imagine that she would have settled down into a traditional way of life. Catherine's children were now six and four years old; they had been denied an aunt who would have been a lively presence in their lives. Catherine had not had the benefit of her sister's support during her pregnancies or the opportunity to share the joy of Christopher and Marianne's arrivals.

Since Ruth died, three of her cousins had married and two had children. Their lives were moving on; hers had been halted. I yearned to see her, to hold her, just to be with her. I felt that I hadn't made any progress, that I was slipping back into a melancholy that had no end.

*

I started preparing the presentation for the conference. I wanted to talk to Jim Fotheringham and Eric Scott about it, and to ask if it would be all right to mention them by name. I also wanted to raise the possibility of making contact with a member of Andrew Steel's family, because I thought it might be helpful to include something about the impact of the murder on his family in my presentation.

Jim had sent me a Christmas card and let me know that he had been ill for some months and had undergone major surgery for cancer in the summer. I had written to him to say how sorry I was to hear of his ordeal. By the time I spoke to him early in the New Year, his health had deteriorated further and he was planning to hand over some of his workload and continue to work only part-time. We had a brief discussion about the implications of meeting a member of Andrew Steel's family, and he said he would make enquiries and get back in touch.

> *14th March 1997*
> *I have had a few thoughts about the issue you mentioned of making contact with Andrew Steel's family. It may be a good thing to do or it may become fraught and tangled. There is an Inner London Probation Service Victims' Service now and I have briefed a senior person there about us all and the tremendous amount of time and energy you put into your preparations for meeting Andy, and what most of us felt to be a good and satisfactory outcome. I would recommend that you call her.*

Jim also said he would contact Andrew Steel's probation officer at the prison to discuss my request with her. Andrew Steel had now left the therapeutic community at Gartree Prison, so Eric was no longer his prison probation officer.

I phoned the Victims' Service and spoke to the senior probation officer. She was busy and due to go on leave, so we arranged a date to meet in May. This meant that there wouldn't be time to include that information in my presentation to the conference, but I decided to go ahead with the meeting.

When I went to the Victims' Service, I expected a short, practical meeting about the way in which an approach could be made to Andrew Steel about my contacting a member of his family, as I knew that Jim had already sent them a detailed briefing.

The office was in a part of London that I didn't know well, so I left home in plenty of time and arrived far too early. I retraced my steps after locating the building and sat in a small café, drinking coffee and going over my reasons for wanting to contact a member of Andrew Steel's family. I still had some ambivalent feelings about my motives and the advisability of making contact. I was conscious that Andrew Steel and his family could see it as an unusual request and might regard it as an intrusion. However, I still wanted to know about the impact of the murder on his family. At the meeting, he had said that his mother had found it difficult to keep in touch with him and that she 'would never forgive him'. I wondered if she would find it helpful to know that although I, too, could not forgive him, I bore no ill will towards him.

The building was in a run-down road where rubbish swirled around in a fitful wind. It was a formidable grey concrete block with a security entryphone. The offices were on an upper floor. I was admitted by the senior probation officer; no other members of staff were in the building.

Two hours later, I emerged feeling that I had been made to go over a lot of unnecessary ground. I had been asked to give an account of events right from the time that the police visited us on the night that Ruth died. Towards the end of the meeting, my reasons for wanting contact with a member of Andrew Steel's family were explored, and I made it clear that I would take no action without his consent. The senior proba-tion officer said she would look into the records and contact me when enquiries had been made.

We then talked in more general terms about the problems that the probation service faced. The responsibility for imple-menting the Victims' Charter for the victims of serious crimes, where a sentence of four years or more was being served, had caused a significant increase in their workload, but they had been given no extra resources. I offered to send her a copy of the presentation I had made to the Bristol conference. This led to her asking if I would be willing to run a workshop at a conference for probation officers on the implementation of the Victims' Charter, to be held in Bournemouth in June. I was pleased to be asked to do this, as I hoped it would help me to understand more about the work of the probation service and its implementation of the Victims' Charter.

*

I didn't find what I expected at the conference. I hadn't realised that each probation service follows its own practice in implementing its statutory duties. The audience was com-posed of staff members from probation services covering the whole of the south of England and South Wales. I assumed that the people who had come to the conference would be more likely to be welcoming of the new work they had been entrusted with under the Victims' Charter.

I sat in on the morning sessions. During the lunch break, I talked to delegates and I encountered a wide range of atti-tudes. Some individual probation officers and services saw the work as a long-overdue recognition of the needs of victims of crime. They were very positive about the probation service being the right statutory agency to undertake this work.

Others were furious, cynical, wary or afraid at the prospect of being involved with the victims of serious crime. Few had had any direct contact with victims; all their previous training and work had been focused on the needs of offenders.

Some services, like the Inner London Probation Service, had already set up specific services for victims; others were training probation officers to take on the role of supporting offenders and victims. Some felt that sending a letter to a victim or victim's family to notify them of the release of the offender fulfilled their statutory duties.

I thought that if such a letter were the only direct contact a victim or a victim's family received from the criminal justice system, it could well feel like an afterthought and might also be very intrusive, as it would arrive without any prior contact or offer of further help. This fired me up for the workshop I was running in the afternoon. I had been asked to cover much the same ground as for the Bristol conference, which I did. However, I put more emphasis on my concerns about a service that had always been entirely offender-orientated now taking on all the needs of victims, and how much would need to be done in training and support for probation officers to enable them to offer an effective service to victims.

It might be very difficult to locate victims or their families. I had wondered how the probation service would have known how to contact us. As far as I knew, we were not listed in the official records; and if I had not wanted to meet Andrew Steel, I might not have realised that the probation service had been given these responsibilities. Some families might vent their long-held frustrations on the hapless probation officer that contacted them, and officers should be prepared for this.

At the end of the session, the discussion was intense, and the group had to be called several times by the organisers to return to the closing plenary session. This conference certainly indicated that there was at least one group of people who needed to understand more about the impact of the criminal justice system on victims and their families.

★

A few days after the conference, I heard from one of Jim's colleagues. He had died in a hospice. I had spoken to him about once a week since he left work in the spring, and although I knew that his cancer was terminal, I was very upset about his death. I sowed a packet of zinnia seeds in our garden in his memory.

★

On 17 August, I received a letter from the Victims' Service. The senior probation officer said she had read the file about Andrew Steel and felt that it would be 'difficult for him to agree that you be put in touch with his family'.

She also revealed that he had had some minor setbacks in his progress through the prison system, and that he might be moved to another prison soon, so I would need to write quickly to his prison probation officer, whose name she gave me.

She commented on the articles in the *Guardian* and *The Times* earlier in the year, writing: 'I am thinking that *he* may wonder when it will end or it what might lead to.' Her letter ended, 'I hope that the contents of this letter are not too dispiriting as it must seem that there are so many "ifs" and "buts" about it all. However you are experienced in dealing with them! Bon courage with your next step!'

The letter made me feel angry and upset. I put it aside for a couple of days before reading it again in case I had misinterpreted or overreacted to what had been written. I reread it: I was still furious. I phoned Roma to see what she thought about it.

Roma's reaction was swift and mirrored my own. She was outraged that the Victims' Service should send a letter that showed more concern for Andrew Steel than for me.

Over the next few days, I drafted and redrafted a response. The first version stated my feelings in no uncertain manner, but I knew I wouldn't send it. The final version was calmer, but still made clear my reactions to the contents of the letter:

28th August 1997

I appreciate the trouble you have gone to in researching the papers about Andrew Steel's family and in contacting his probation officer at Gartree Prison.

However, I do have a number of concerns about your letter and felt it was best to write to you so that you have the opportunity to consider them. In fact I was quite upset after reading and rereading your letter which is why I have waited before responding.

PROCESS

It is now nearly seven months since I first raised the possibility of meeting with a member of Andrew Steel's family. I was referred by Eric to Jim and from Jim to yourself. Now your advice is contact the PO at Gartree. With respect, I wonder what you feel has been achieved by the involvement of the Victims' Service? I feel that the time from my point of view has not been used productively and I am back where I started. And now you are telling me that I have to act quickly as he will be transferred soon.

BOUNDARIES

When we met in May, I thought I had made it clear that I had chosen to request an approach through a third party so that he had the opportunity to discuss the request with someone who knows him and something about his family. He can then make his decision, which of course I would respect. It would have been easy for me to write to Andrew Steel or indeed to trace and contact his family directly. I could be wrong but it seems as if a lot of assumptions are being made while Andrew Steel doesn't even know the request has been made.

PUBLICITY

It is unfortunate if Andrew Steel has been upset by publicity but your comment 'I am thinking that he may wonder when it will end', together with other comments in your letter, made me feel that you had more concern for his needs than mine. I have never mentioned his name and have always made it a condition of giving interviews that the journalist does not print his name. You will know that this information is in the public domain and so I have been very careful in selecting which requests to respond to.

I have turned down many requests for interviews. I have also advised the prison in advance of any publicity and indeed have been asked by the probation service at the prison to be interviewed about the meeting for a local paper.

Overall, I was left feeling that it would be a relief if I gave up and shut up.

However experienced I have had to become in dealing with the criminal justice system I still resent the unnecessary time and emotional energy it takes to achieve anything.

I realise that you are coping with an enormous workload and also that you and your colleagues are setting up a new service but I had hoped that the Victims' Service would have been able to offer some ongoing support if a meeting were to take place.

Several weeks later, I had a phone call from her. She said she was sorry that I had been upset and that her letter had been written under pressure of time. After further discussion,

I still felt that she didn't fully understand how let down I felt by my first encounter with a statutory service that was, after all, supposed to be there for me and not for Andrew Steel. My disquiet over the probation service taking responsibility for the needs of victims was reinforced.

My attempt to meet a member of Andrew Steel's family was developing into an echo of the drawn-out process to meet him. I telephoned the prison probation officer and she said she would be willing to discuss my request with Andrew Steel and that it would help her if I could write to her setting out my reasons for wanting to make contact with a member of his family.

In the autumn, I was approached by BBC South East, who wanted me to take part in a programme they were making about restorative justice. They had already filmed some of the work being done by the Thames Valley Police with young offenders. After seeing Andrew Steel, I had agreed to notify the prison about any publicity, so I wrote again to the prison probation officer.

I am writing to let you know that a programme about Restorative Justice will be screened by BBC South East on Thursday 20th November in the First Sight series. I was interviewed for the programme but don't know if anything will actually appear in the screened version as the production team had twelve and a half hours of filming, covering many locations and people to edit into a half-hour programme.

While writing, I wonder if you have yet been able to discuss my request with Andrew Steel.

Nine months after writing to Eric in February to ask if it would be possible to contact a member of Andrew Steel's family, I received a letter from his prison probation officer:

3rd November 1997

Thank you for your recent letter regarding contact with Andrew Steel's family.

I've spoken to Andy twice about your request, but he feels unable to contact his family about your request.

Unfortunately, Andy feels that he needs to concentrate on getting through his sentence and has requested me to ask that you don't attempt to contact him again in the immediate future.

I understand that this will be a disappointment for you, but feel I must respect his wishes, and not press him to reconsider. He understands that you have no wish to add to his problems, but has asked that I keep his whereabouts confidential when he moves from Gartree.

I wish you the very best for the future.

I could have been told this months before and been spared the upset with the Victims' Service. I was relieved that I would no longer know where Andrew Steel was, but this was counter-balanced by the impression that he just wanted to keep his head down and do his time, and had therefore rejected my request.

Chapter Twenty

Celeste

I RECEIVED AN E-MAIL from Pat Bane, the director of Murder Victims' Families for Reconciliation, just before Christmas 1997. We had both spoken at the LifeLines conference in Edinburgh in 1995 and had kept in touch from time to time ever since.

The news it contained was startling.

> *We recently made a trip to Oklahoma with several MVFR members to do some public education and to begin forming a chapter there. One of the speakers was Celeste Dixon, a young woman whose mother was murdered. While we've talked on the phone for a long time, I had never met her personally. When I heard her speak for the first time, I was surprised to hear her say that a man named Micheal Richard had killed her mother. She first favored the death penalty but has gotten past that and now is interested in learning more about Micheal and possibly contacting him.*

Pat went on to say that she had given Celeste my postal address, and gave me Celeste's postal and e-mail addresses.

It seemed strange that I should hear from a member of the Dixon family just after my attempt to make contact with a member of Andrew Steel's family had come to nothing. Although I wanted to contact Celeste straight away, I first had to let Micheal know about the request and find out how he felt about it. Christmas was going to be hard for him. His brother, Scott, had been murdered in the summer. He had written: 'The death of my only brother has truly brought a lot of things to the surface for me and for the first time in my life I experienced a pain that I had never known and I know that this pain will never vanish until I talk with the woman that caused his death and it's not that I hate this woman. She has to face her own demons and I know that she is hurting also, because I know that I have been suffering for many years.' Also, by the end of 1997, thirty-seven men had been executed at the prison in Texas — half of the United States total executions for the year. I didn't want Micheal to receive the letter during the holiday period, so I waited a week and then wrote to him about Pat's e-mail.

I have sent an e-mail to Pat saying that while I would be willing to help Celeste, I don't want to contact her before asking you if you have any problems with that. You are my first concern and I don't want to do anything behind your back or anything that would not be right for you.

It would be really helpful if you could let me know quickly but I feel bad putting pressure on you when I know things are very hard for you at present. However, I had to let you know as you may want to hear from Celeste Dixon and this is the only way you will know of her interest.

I walked to the post box nearest to our home and put the letter through the slit on Christmas Eve after the last collection had been taken. Catherine and her family were coming to us for Christmas Day, so as soon as I got home I was going to start the food preparations. When I opened the front door, there was a pile of post on the mat, mostly decorated with Christmas stickers. I riffled through the envelopes; there was one from the United States with the name Celeste Dixon and a return address in the top left-hand corner.

Inside the envelope were five sheets of lightweight blue paper. I sat down to read by the light of the decorations on our Christmas tree.

Dear Lesley

*I got your address from Pat Bane, who may have already written to you
to explain my connection to you.*

*I understand that you have been the pen pal of a death row inmate in
Texas named Micheal Richard. Pat told me that you had even gone to
Houston for his retrial in 1995 and stayed with his sister.*

*I'm sure you know the name of the victim in his case — Marguerite
Dixon. My name is Celeste Dixon and she was my mother.*

*When this first happened in 1986, I was, obviously very, very angry
and full of hate for Micheal. Pat told me that your daughter had been
murdered so I'm sure you can understand what I went through. When
the prosecutors told us they were going for the death penalty I never
even questioned it. At the time I could have killed him myself. In fact,
I went to that first trial in August 1987 with the ultimate goal of hearing
the judge pronounce the sentence of death.*

*Any other outcome was unthinkable to me and my entire family.
Implied, but never spoken by the prosecution was the promise that having Micheal die would be a fair compensation to us for the loss of our
mother. This was supposed to make us feel better.*

*After the trial, though, I was standing in the hallway outside the
courtroom with my family, we were all happy because we had gotten
what we wanted. But I happened to look over at Micheal's mother and
just for that particular instant she happened to be standing alone. And
she was sobbing. My heart went out to her and without stopping to think
about it I walked over to her and hugged her. I realised then that she
would feel the loss of her son just as keenly as we had felt the loss of our
mother.*

*That incident started me thinking about capital punishment over
the next year. By the time I started classes at the University of Texas at
Austin in the fall of 1988 I had come to the conclusion that capital
punishment was wrong.*

The main thing I saw wrong with it is that it would not bring my mother back but it would cause another family to lose someone they loved, spreading more grief and suffering to others. In fact, the only difference I could see between my mother's death and Micheal's death, when the sentence is finally carried out, is that his family will have years to agonize over the loss, where my family had to deal with it suddenly. But the results will be the same, someone will deliberately take another human being's life.

When I began to see capital punishment in that light I realized that by supporting the death penalty I was actively wishing for another human being to die. And I didn't like the way that made me feel, because I felt that didn't make me any better than the person who actually pulls the trigger. It's an old, sometimes trite saying but 'two wrongs don't make a right' is appropriate in this case.

I went along for about six years thinking that not wishing Micheal to die was all that was required of me. In 1994 I went on a retreat and after reading the story of St Maria Goretti I realized that I also had to forgive Micheal for what he had done.

Initially, that forgiveness was for me. By letting go of all my anger and hatred I was finally able to get rid of the intense pain that always accompanied my memories and thoughts of my mother. Forgiving helped me first of all, to heal my wounds. Lately, though I've come to realize that Micheal needs to have that forgiveness as well. It has helped me, now it's time to help him. I think he needs to know that at least one member of the Dixon family doesn't hate him and isn't waiting for him to die. I'm planning to write him a letter and let him know how I feel. I'm hoping to get it mailed to him before Christmas.

The reason I am writing to you is simply to establish contact with someone who knows Micheal. I don't think it was an accident that I mentioned Micheal's name in front of Pat. Once she heard it she knew he must be the same person you are writing to.

If you feel that it wouldn't be a violation of Micheal's trust, maybe you could tell me something about him. What is he like, how did you *first get to know him, etc. Of course, if you feel that's something private between the two of you I understand that and respect it.*

At any rate, I would like to maybe get to know you, if you are willing to write me back.

Right now I'm doing seasonal work for the National Park Service, which means I move around about every six months so my mail is sent to one of my sisters.

If you attended the entire trial then I'm sure you saw her there. She and my other sister were the ones who found my mom.

I hope to hear from you sometime in the future.

Sincerely

Celeste Dixon

It was such a powerful letter that I needed to read it several times to take in the information and the responses it aroused. Here was a young woman who had been on a much longer journey than I had. Her mother died in 1986; she had been pro capital punishment and now was moving towards offering forgiveness to Micheal. I had always been anti capital punishment, even in my darkest moments. I tried to think how Micheal would react. I knew that he had always wanted to contact the Dixon family to express his feelings about his actions and to acknowledge the suffering he had caused them.

Her assumption that Micheal would be executed brought home even more sharply the cruelty of capital punishment. Indeed his family would have more to suffer, and the many years of uncertainty made it a long-drawn-out process. Celeste didn't know that the Richard family were now grieving for Scott, so that they now had experienced both sides of murder.

I was glad I had written to Micheal before I received Celeste's letter; I didn't know if I would have been able to hold back from telling him that she wanted to forgive him.

Still pondering these issues, I had to start the preparations for our family Christmas. Dishes and cutlery not in everyday use to be got out of cupboards, vegetables prepared to go in the fridge overnight, stuffing to prepare for the turkey. As I did this I listened, as I have nearly every year of my life, to the carol concert from King's College, Cambridge. The familiar strains of 'Once in Royal David's City' and other carols and the readings accompanied my routine tasks.

In the New Year, I watched the post each day hoping for a letter from Micheal, and in the middle of January 1998 his familiar writing appeared on an envelope.

I want you to know that if you had given Celeste Dixon my address I wouldn't have minded, because I would like to talk with her and I've asked my lawyer if I could write to someone in the Dixon family to let them know that if I could go back and change things I would, so if she wants to contact me I don't mind. . . . I would like to get to know this lady and I want you to let her know it's ok to write or come and visit anytime that she wants and I'll tell her anything she wants to know about me and my life.

He had been ill and on lockdown, which meant that he had been isolated, alone for over twenty-three hours a day, with none of his personal belongings. Despite this, he was cheerful as he had a new pen friend, this time not through LifeLines. He had been helping an illiterate man on the Row by writing letters for him and had asked if he, too, could write to the man's pen friend, Sian. Micheal asked me to contact Sian and send her a copy of a photograph taken of him when I went to Texas.

I wrote a long letter to Celeste that evening. I told her how I first got in touch with Micheal, meeting him and his family in 1995 at the retrial, the impressions I had formed of him during our seven-year friendship and enclosing some press cuttings of interviews about Micheal and our correspondence. I asked her if, when she wrote to Micheal, she would include the description of her going to hug his mother, Louella, at the end of the first trial.

We started to correspond by e-mail and by post, exchanging information about our families, our work and ourselves.

By mid-January, I had talked about Celeste's letter with a number of friends, including the founder of LifeLines, Jan Arriens. Jan has to deal with a lot of the heartache that comes with the penfriendships that are ended by execution. He was delighted to hear some good news. A few days later, he phoned to ask if I would be willing to take part in a programme with Celeste on the BBC World Service about the death penalty in the United States. Texas was planning to execute a woman, Karla Faye Tucker. Because no state had executed a woman for many years, the media were following her case closely. I telephoned Celeste, so that the first time we spoke to each other wouldn't be during a live broadcast. It was lovely to hear her warm Texan voice so clearly. This brief conversation made me feel even closer to her.

When I arrived at Bush House in late January for the recording, the interviewer was playing back the tape of an interview she had done with an American lawyer earlier that day. The lawyer was anti capital punishment but held out no hope of a stay of execution for Karla Faye Tucker. The execution was due to take place the following week.

Karla Faye Tucker was executed on 3 February. The media interest was intense, in sharp contrast to the lack of interest in the thirty-seven men who had died at the same prison in Texas in 1997.

A few days later, another long letter arrived from Celeste with a copy of the letter she had sent to Micheal. She told me more about her mother and how she had found the Texan climate, with its two seasons of 'very hot' and 'very hot and humid' weather, hard to bear. The family had decided that Mrs Dixon should be buried in her home state of West Virginia, where the weather had real seasons.

Celeste works for the U.S. Parks Service and is a great Civil War buff – I had already learned a lot about the battlefields from her. She had worked at the Chickamauga Battlefield in Georgia throughout the previous summer, and in the winter she had been based at the home of Harry S. Truman, the American president who served two terms of office just after the Second World War. She asked me to tell her about Ruth.

Celeste's letter to Micheal got straight down to its purpose after identifying herself and how she had got in touch with him.

I am writing to tell you that I forgive you for the death of my mother.
Eleven years ago I would never have thought that what I am doing now
was even remotely possible, but things change. This has not been an
easy thing for me to do, and it's definitely been a very long and difficult
path to get here, so I think I should explain how it all came about.

She had been serving in the U.S. Navy and was based in Puerto Rico when the news of her mother's death came through. She was given a brief home leave and then had to return to complete her service.

The trial was held a year after her mother's death and she and her family attended, waiting for and wanting to hear the death penalty announced. When Celeste learned more about Micheal's life, she started to see that he was someone beyond the person who had taken her mother's life. This and the insight into his family's feelings gained when they gave evidence started her on the path towards forgiveness. It had been a long path and not an easy one. On a retreat in 1994, she had picked up a book from the library shelves about the lives of Catholic women saints. She read of Maria Goretti, a young Italian woman, who had been raped and seriously injured, and who had forgiven her attacker before she died. He served a long prison sentence, and on his release he went to see Maria's mother and asked for her forgiveness. Maria was made a saint and the man and her mother went to Rome together for the ceremony.

Maria's story was a key turning point for Celeste. Now she had to struggle with the prospect of being in touch with Micheal.

Micheal was thrilled to receive Celeste's letter:

I was very surprised in just what I read and thanked God for such a blessing and I wrote her back and she should have received it by now and I hope to hear from her again.

Chapter Twenty-one

Forgiveness

CELESTE'S ACCOUNT of her journey towards forgiveness
stirred up a lot of feelings in me. I admired what she had done
and wished so much that I could get to the same destination.
What was it that held me back? What was so different about
our situations? I had had the advantage of meeting Andrew
Steel; but she had heard far more about Micheal at the original trial than I knew even now about Andrew Steel.

I brooded, read books and articles about forgiveness, and
became more and more despondent. I wasn't sure any more
what forgiveness really meant. The dictionary definitions I
looked up talked about ceasing to feel angry or resentful
towards an offender. I had always distinguished in my mind
between what Andrew Steel did and who he was. I hadn't felt
anger towards him, but overwhelming sadness at what he
had done. Christian texts were full of well-known admonish-
ments, many of which I had dutifully chanted as a child at
school and in church: 'And forgive us our trespasses, as we
forgive those that trespass against us.' And from the Creed: 'I
believe in the forgiveness of sins.'

I talked with friends about how I was feeling. Some put
forward the idea that forgiveness is God's responsibility. That
seems to me a separate issue: if people believe in a God, then
they can ask for forgiveness for themselves, as Micheal had
done. For me, that didn't take away from the people affected
by it the onus of forgiving the perpetrator of a crime.

Alexander Pope famously said, 'To err is human, to forgive, divine.' Perhaps I would not be able to forgive. In many

ways, I felt that it wasn't my place. If Andrew Steel needed to seek anyone's forgiveness, it was Ruth's. For me even to be considering forgiving him myself felt like a betrayal of her.

*

I was going around in non-productive circles. I felt that I needed to talk to someone not directly affected by it all and so I approached a long-standing member of my Quaker Meeting. When I first met Bettina, I had found her rather intimidating, but she had been very kind to me after Ruth's death, and had come to the funeral. She agreed to meet me, and we shared lunch at her home. I took a small saffron cake as a gift and found that we have common Cornish roots.

I poured out my confusion and distress about not being able to forgive Andrew Steel. I mentioned a number of Quaker writers who had written about forgiveness – the message was clear, as in other faiths and philosophies, that it was the *right* thing to do. She listened intently, sitting upright in a high-backed chair with her hands in a steeple under her chin. As I finished speaking, she closed her eyes and remained silent for several minutes. When she reopened her eyes and spoke, what she said surprised me. 'I don't think any of the people you have been reading have had the extremity of your situation in mind when they were writing.'

She felt I had gone a long way towards forgiveness by not wanting to harm Andrew Steel, and wanting him to be able to get on with his life in a constructive way when he is released. No one can 'make' themselves feel something. Either you do or you don't. Forgiveness may come or it may not. Other people had said that they felt I was being very hard on myself. Perhaps I should let the issue rest where it was.

Chapter Twenty-two

Meeting Celeste and seeing a play

IN MARCH 1998, Jan Arriens phoned to say that a speaker for the LifeLines conference in May had had to cancel because she was involved in a long-running trial in the United States. It was a special conference for LifeLines, marking the tenth anniversary of its formation, to be held at Cambridge Friends Meeting House, the venue for the first ever conference.

He wondered if Celeste would be willing to come to Cambridge and make a presentation. We knew she had spoken for MVFR in the United States. Her letters and the short broadcast we had done together confirmed that she was a natural communicator. She responded quickly that she would like to come but would have to check with her employers to ask if she could be released. She had only just moved back to the Georgia battlefields for the summer season. Her boss agreed that she could take five days' leave, which would give her three complete days in England, including the day of the conference.

I wanted to invite Celeste to stay with us for at least part of her visit, but was anxious about Vic's response. When I asked him, he hesitated, then said, 'Well, I suppose I can wear it.' Not one for overstatement, this meant 'Yes'.

E-mails flashed to and fro with increasing intensity. We wanted Celeste to pack as much as possible into her first visit to England, particularly to show her sites connected with the Plantagenet kings, her special period of interest in English history.

We agreed to meet her at Gatwick on Thursday morning.

She would stay with us on Thursday night, go to Cambridge for Friday night and return home with me at the end of the conference on Saturday. We would go to Canterbury on Sunday, and on Monday she would catch her return flight to the United States.

Jan asked me to introduce Celeste at the conference and explain how we had been put in touch. He also asked if I would be willing to be interviewed for an article about LifeLines to appear in the *Guardian* during the week of the conference. Celeste would be interviewed, by e-mail rather than by phone.

*

Early in May, I was contacted by a friend whose son had worked with the actress Anita Dobson, who was currently appearing in a play at the Birmingham Repertory Theatre. *Frozen*, by Briony Lavery, was about a woman whose daughter had been murdered and who had been to see the offender in prison. My friend asked: 'Has this been based on your experience?' I hadn't heard about the play but was interested in finding out more. She put me in touch with Anita Dobson, who told me that on one evening there would be discussions with the author and director of the play and with the cast before and after the performance. I phoned a friend who lives near Worcester and asked if she would be interested in going. She already had the flyer by her telephone and had been thinking of going to see the play, but didn't want to go by herself.

On the train to Birmingham, I thought with growing excitement and some trepidation about Celeste's visit in two days' time. Although we had written to each other and spoken on the telephone, I wasn't sure what her expectations would be. I had seen the draft of the article for the *Guardian*, due to be published on the day of Celeste's arrival. Towards the end of the article, there was a quote from Celeste:

> 'I sort of think of Lesley as a mother figure,' Dixon says. 'I
> don't have any other mother figure in my life right now.'

Several people had already commented to both Celeste and
myself that our coming together meant that Celeste had a
new mother and I had a new daughter. Some people, seeking
a 'happy ending', had told me that I had a new daughter to
replace Ruth. I found these comments sentimental and un-
helpful. Thankfully, I knew that Celeste did not mean that
she saw me as a substitute for her mother, and I certainly didn't
want to her to feel that she had in any way to replace Ruth.

Our relationship was complex, with many uncomfortable
areas. How would she feel when she saw the letters I had
received from Micheal and the folder of photographs and
cuttings about him that I had prepared for the conference?

We were both alone in our families in our attitudes
towards the person who had taken the life of our relation.
Her family didn't even know she was coming to England.

★

My friend met me at Birmingham New Street station. Our
seats in the modern and airy theatre were in a prime position.
We saw in the programme that the offender was described as a
paedophile who had murdered a number of young girls. The
presentations, the questions from the audience and discussion before the performance centred almost entirely on the
paedophilia aspect of the play. I turned to my friend and whispered, 'But he *killed* them.'

The stage setting was simple; there were only three main
characters. Anita Dobson played the part of Nancy, a mother
whose youngest daughter, Rhona, had disappeared twenty

years before. Ralph, the paedophile and murderer, was shown both as a free man and as a prisoner. He showed little insight into his behaviour, and no remorse. The third character was an American psychologist working with Ralph to explore the reasons for his actions.

Nancy decides that she wants to meet Ralph. The psychiatrist thinks that such a meeting would not be beneficial.

I was transfixed by Anita Dobson's performance as her character moved through a succession of powerful emotions. In the first act, a scene in her daughter's bedroom shows that Rhona's possessions have not been put away; a collection of nature-study items are still on a table in her bedroom. Nancy cleans the room and recalls the journey they had shared to the Brecon Beacons when they found a piece of gorse with sheep's wool caught in it.

Nancy becomes involved with an organisation of parents of missing children and finds she enjoys public speaking. Then, twenty years after Rhona's disappearance, Ralph is arrested. Rhona's skeleton is found with those of other children Ralph had raped and killed, and Nancy and her elder daughter, Ingrid, go to the mortuary. They take the piece of gorse and other mementos to put in the small box containing Rhona's remaining bones.

Leaving the mortuary, Nancy and Ingrid go to a small park where Ingrid advises her mother to 'let go and move on'. She says they have to forgive Ralph with all their hearts, and that Nancy should go to see him and tell him so. Nancy isn't ready for this course of action and responds angrily that she would like to torture and kill him – 'She was my little girl!' Ingrid responds, 'So was I.' And the first act ends.

Although the second act included Nancy's visit to see Ralph at the prison, it was the end of the first act that made the most impact on me. Did Catherine feel that she had lost not only her sister but my love and support as well? After all, who can compete with a dead sister in seeking attention from a grieving mother? Had I been so taken up with my own sorrow and trying to get information that she felt neglected? She is rather like Vic in that she deals with her emotional life inwardly, rather than by talking very much about her feelings. She had also had a lot to cope with after the birth of her two children within sixteen months. Although we had talked about Ruth, it was mainly to share the happy memories. The ripples arising from Ruth's death moved not only through space, but also through time.

I didn't sleep much that night. The words 'So was I' reverberated in the darkness.

*

The next day, back at home, I again rechecked the room I had prepared for Celeste, putting some flowers from our garden and a welcoming card on the small table by the bed in the bedroom that had been Catherine's. Vic and I had an early night and got up at 4 a.m. to be on the road in time to get to Gatwick to meet Celeste. We were there in good time and I bought three copies of the *Guardian*, one for Celeste, one to send to Micheal and one for me. I skimmed through the article. There was no address for LifeLines given: a great disappointment, as the aim of the publicity had been to recruit new members so that all those on Death Row who wanted a pen friend could have one.

I had prepared a small board with Celeste's name on it surrounded by smiley-face stickers, and scanned the faces eagerly as the people from the flight emerged from the customs hall. She spotted me first. She was shorter and had lighter hair than I expected. We hugged, then went to put her luggage in our car. At a nearby hotel, we had breakfast together, then travelled back along the now crowded M25.

Vic left for work soon after we got home and Celeste said she thought she should get some sleep. She had worked a full day before leaving and hadn't been able to sleep much on the flight. We agreed that I would wake her in three hours.

The weather was wonderful. After she got up, we sat outside and looked at photographs. Celeste had brought photographs of her family and her work and I passed her the folder with the photographs of Micheal and his family. She looked through them slowly, asking me to identify the members of the family that she didn't recognise. With a sigh she closed the folder and said she was awake enough to go to Hatfield House for the rest of the afternoon.

The next day we went to London for her 'tourist's day'. We put her overnight bag in the left-luggage at King's Cross, then went to the Tower of London. I had not been there for many years, and was pleased to find a re-enactment taking place in one of the buildings, with people dressed in period costume talking about the Tower in the time of Edward III. Next we took a river boat to Westminster, were disappointed to find that Parliament was not open but looked around Westminster Abbey and found the tombs of Queen Elizabeth I and Mary, Queen of Scots. It was a hot day and we were both tired by the late afternoon, so we took a taxi back to King's Cross; I tried to give a lightning commentary on the sights as we drove through the gathering rush-hour traffic. We got on the same train but I got off at my home station, while Celeste travelled on to Cambridge to be met by Jan.

Next morning, on the way to Cambridge, I reviewed the brief introduction I had been asked to make to Celeste's presentation. It explained the extraordinary way Celeste and I had come into contact, and our links with Micheal.

The morning speaker was a mental-health expert who works with death-row prisoners in California. She illustrated her presentation with case histories and charts showing the relationship between life experiences and crime. She outlined six key factors. The more of these that a person had experienced, the more likely they were to become involved in crime. They were:

—Severe marital distress in the parents' marriage
—Low socio-economic status
—Large families, overcrowding
—Paternal criminality
—Maternal psychiatric disorder
—Being fostered or in an out-of-home placement

Micheal had experienced all six; and I realised that I had four in my own childhood. The missing factors for me were that my father was not a criminal and I didn't come from a large family.

After lunch, Celeste spoke extempore, powerfully, and although we had already exchanged a lot of information before and since her arrival, I learned more about the situation in the United States. She said that if Micheal had been charged in any other county than Harris County in Texas, he would have received a term sentence rather than the death penalty, because he had gone to her parents' home to steal and with no intention of harming anybody.

As I walked down the stairs for the tea break, a woman stopped me and said, 'I take it that you have forgiven the man who killed your daughter?' When I told her that I had not been able to do so, she challenged me fiercely. I was taken aback, not expecting this from a member of LifeLines. I found it very difficult to respond to her. She kept insisting that there was a fundamental inconsistency in my writing to Micheal without having forgiven Andrew Steel. In the end, I said it was difficult for me to explain and for her to understand, as she wasn't in my situation. I found this encounter very upsetting and felt rattled for the rest of the day and evening.

★

Next morning, Vic drove Celeste and me to Canterbury. Many years before, I had sung with a choir in the cathedral. We had moved in procession along the cloisters and into the cathedral, awed by the space encompassed in the soaring arches, the light streaming through the brightly coloured windows and the sound of our voices echoing against the stone. Celeste and I looked around the cathedral and decided to attend a service in the late afternoon. The choir moved into their stalls; the congregation sat in pews nearby. The content of the service resonated with references to our shared experiences and particularly to Micheal's situation on Death Row. Psalm 107 included the line: 'Such as sit in darkness and in the shadow of death, being bound in affliction and iron.' The Old Testament reading was about redemption; the New Testament one about resurrection.

On our way home, we visited Vic's niece, Teresa, who had given birth to a daughter, Eloise, earlier that week. It was lovely to see her, her beautiful baby and proud partner, but I felt, as I have felt when other nieces have had their babies, very emotional and conscious that Ruth would almost certainly have had a family by now.

Next morning, Catherine came to our house, and she and Celeste were able to have a short time together before the journey to Gatwick. Throughout Celeste's visit the weather had been unseasonably hot; she had seen England at its best, the countryside fresh and bright with unfurling leaves and flowers. Now she had a long journey home to face and she would have to go straight back to work the following morning.

I wrote to Micheal when I got home to tell him about Celeste's visit, and sent him a copy of the order of service from Canterbury Cathedral.

Chapter Twenty-three
The future

OUT OF THE BLUE, a letter arrived from the senior probation officer at the Inner London Probation Service Victims' Service. It was addressed to me; Vic wasn't mentioned.

14th August 1998

I have been checking as to when Andrew Steel's first parole review takes place and it seems that it is due in February 2000. This as you know is not when he can be released as his tariff does not expire until 2003. However, his progress will be considered and they will review how far he has succeeded in following his sentence plan and whether he could in future be considered for open conditions.

The reports for the Parole Review will be compiled in the last quarter of 1999 and I will be in touch with you then. At that point it will be possible for you to make representations to the Parole Board and express concerns about his future release. I am enclosing a leaflet which explains this.

I am sure that this brings you more thoughts about how time is going on and how the system continues in a rather inexorable way. I thought it best to give you as much notice as possible of the next stages as I know we have not discussed this before.

I hope things continue well in your various enterprises.

The leaflet set out information about life sentences for victims and their families. I learned that probation officers now have a statutory duty to contact victims' families within two months of any trial that results in a life sentence. It is now possible for families to get information about the length of the sentence. Contact will be made again by the probation service three years before the end of the sentence so that the parole board can take victims' views into account. It is good to know that more information and involvement is being offered to victims and their families.

By November 1999, the Victims' Service still hadn't contacted me, so I decided to phone. I asked them if they could ensure that the letter, when it was sent, would be addressed to both Vic and myself. A letter, from another officer, arrived in the week before Christmas and said that Hertfordshire Probation Service had been asked to arrange to visit us prior to the parole-board review to be held in February.

On contacting the Victims' Service, I was told that their normal practice was to transfer the responsibility for contacting victims' families to the probation service covering the area where the family lives. The explanation for the delay, they said, was because I had contacted the Inner London Probation Service about the possibility of meeting a member of Andrew Steel's family.

With the Christmas and Millennium New Year holidays about to start, I didn't expect that the Hertfordshire Probation Service would be in touch until January. I tried not to think about it, but with the tenth anniversary of Ruth's death rapidly approaching, it was hard not to be thinking about how our lives had been when she was with us for her last Christmas and New Year in 1989. So full of life, so full of promise and so much a vital part of our family. In the intervening years, most of her cousins had developed their careers, had married or were in established partnerships, and some had children. Family celebrations and sorrows had been shared without Ruth, and her absence coloured these events.

On Millennium Eve, our grandchildren came to stay with us overnight. Catherine and Stephen were going to London to see the fireworks. Christopher and Marianne went to bed at their usual times and we promised to wake them at 11.30 p.m. They came downstairs and we sat together watching the television coverage of the celebrations around the world until the early hours of 2000.

Three weeks into January, we had heard nothing from the Hertfordshire Probation Service. I phoned the county offices and spoke to someone who responded sympathetically and promptly, promising that someone would be in touch before the end of the working day. A senior probation officer phoned and arranged to come to our house on 28 January. Much to my delight, Vic said that although he didn't see much point in him being present, as his view was that a life sentence should mean just that, if I wanted him to be there, he would be.

The senior probation officer was a bluff middle-aged man who quickly established his credentials. He had been a member of parole boards as well as having life-sentence prisoners on his caseload and making contact with the families of murder victims. He had been given no date for the parole-board meeting. He hadn't been sent all the papers and so had very little information on what had happened. We had to explain the background.

He listened intently, drawing out our differing views and explaining that policy changes meant that life-sentence prisoners now have to 'prove' that they are capable of leading a non-violent life before even being considered for release and that few are now released at the expiry of their sentence. From the little he had seen of the case, he felt it was unlikely that the parole board would approve a move to the rehabilitative part of the sentence, and so Andrew Steel would be in prison for longer than thirteen years. In his experience, the longer someone was in prison, the harder it was to adjust to a new life after prison.

My major concern was that Andrew Steel had a previous history of violence to women but had no criminal record for these incidents as no charges had been made. If the parole board only saw information about the trial, they could make an assumption that his attack on Ruth was a one-off event, as there would be no record of his previous violence. Given that his violence was directed towards women, it was difficult to see how a judgement could be made about his behaviour when he had spent the past ten years in a predominantly male environment. However, if it was felt that he presented no future threat, my view was still that he should be released after completing the rehabilitative part of his sentence. Even after release, life-sentence prisoners are closely monitored and can be recalled to prison if their behaviour presents any cause for concern.

I had already found out that offenders are entitled to see all the reports that go to the parole board, and I felt uncomfortable about Andrew Steel seeing that despite my views on rehabilitation, it could be my comments that prompted an investigation of his previous history of violence. And yet I felt I had to express my concern. Any possibility of him hurting anyone else on being released was too awful to contemplate.

The probation officer said that he would check the report that the police would have made following the trial to see if they had included any information about Andrew Steel's previous violent behaviour. He would be back in touch to let us know about the outcome of the parole-board review.

After the probation officer left, Vic and I agreed that it had given us an opportunity, as was our right, to talk to someone from the criminal justice system. But I couldn't help reflecting that ten years was a long time to wait.

When I contacted family members to let them know about

the meeting, a variety of views were expressed, but most of them were relieved to learn that Andrew Steel was not likely to be let out of prison in 2003. 'I hope he never comes out' was a comment uttered more than once.

Vic, Catherine and I went together to the crematorium five days after this meeting on the tenth anniversary of Ruth's death. We took a bouquet of blue and white flowers to place in the area where her ashes were scattered and walked in the grounds for half an hour. We spent the rest of the day together, a rare treat for us to have time with Catherine by herself, because of her family and work commitments. We took her home in time to pick up the children from school, where Christopher burst out of the door, rushed up to me and said, 'Today is the tenth anniversary of Ruth Moreland's death.' Catherine had told both children that we might be upset when we met them and the reasons why. When we got back to their home, he asked lots of questions and, as is common with most nine-year-olds, he was most interested in the physical details, as indeed Ruth was at the same age. His directness was refreshing and he got clear answers from us. Nearby, Marianne was listening intently.

The probation officer contacted us again later in the week saying that there was nothing in the police report and it would be helpful if I could make contact with one of the police officers. I was able to do this, as I had kept in touch with Geoff Parratt, now retired after a long career in the force. He also confirmed that no release date would be considered at the parole-board meeting, though he still didn't have a date for the meeting.

The term used to describe the situation when someone's sentence is extended is 'knocked back'. 'Knocked over' might be more appropriate; it seems that Andrew Steel's situation is becoming more like Micheal's, except that he doesn't have the threat of execution hanging over him. I have become aware that our encounters with the criminal justice system are going to extend further into the future as we will be contacted every time the parole board meet, which is likely to be every two years.

*

Micheal is now in the fifteenth year of his imprisonment. In Texas, more than 220 people have been executed since he arrived on Death Row. As governor of Texas, George W. Bush signed far more death warrants than any other state governor. There are signs that there is growing unease with the death penalty in the United States. This follows the certain knowledge that some people who were innocent have been convicted and executed – this was a key factor in repealing capital punishment in the UK in 1965.

At the end of 1999, Micheal was transferred to a new facility where the regime is even harsher. Many of his personal possessions were taken away from him before the move. He spends most of time in a cell with no natural light or soft surfaces. The Texan climate means that he spends much of the year feeling unbearably hot or unbearably cold. In a recent letter, he said, 'I need something to do around here, because I know every spot on this wall like the back of my hand.'

*

Celeste and I are still in touch, regularly by e-mail but we also write letters as we both like to receive post. We both enjoy reading and recommend books to each other. She often sends me postcards when she is on her travels and my knowledge of American Civil War history has been greatly extended by her enthusiasm. Earlier this year, her post with the U.S. Parks Service was made permanent, and she is currently working at the family home of Dr Martin Luther King. She sounds happy and fulfilled in her work and is looking forward to developing her career.

*

Vic retired at the end of 1998 from the job he had held for twenty-five years. We have adjusted, with few problems, to sharing our home now we are both in the house more than we used to be. However, we are both working freelance, so the house has had to adjust, too, with two 'offices' created – mine in the bedroom that used to be Ruth's and Vic's in an alcove in the dining room. His way of coping with the aftermath of Ruth's death has been different to my own, but it is just as valid and I am very proud of him.

We are looking forward to a holiday together in the Isles of Scilly with Catherine and her family. Marianne asked me if she and I can have a day together to do some painting. I said, 'That's a lovely idea. Do you know what you want to paint?' 'Yes,' she said promptly, 'I'd like to go to Auntie Ruth's seat on St Martin's.'

I still struggle with the issue of forgiveness; it doesn't dominate my life, but it niggles away in the background. I don't cry so often now, but my heart still contracts painfully if, while we are eating our evening meal, the doorbell rings.

Epilogue

SOME YEARS AFTER Ruth died, I met a woman I knew on a train. Her daughter and Ruth had been at the same primary school together, but she and her family had moved away to another town some years before.

'How are Catherine and Ruth?' she asked. I told her that Catherine was happily married with two children and living about half an hour north of us. I continued, 'You can't have heard our sad news,' and explained that Ruth had died in 1990.

The woman was very shocked to hear this and even more so when I told her that Ruth had been murdered. She asked lots of questions, which I replied to briefly, conscious of the listening fellow passengers.

After taking in the information, she summarised: 'Ruth was killed by someone she knew, who used a knife; he was arrested and is now serving a life sentence and there was nothing in the news about it. So, it was just an ordinary murder.'

Acknowledgements

LIKE MANY PEOPLE, I had often thought about writing a book. But *An Ordinary Murder* is not the book I planned to write or would ever have wanted to write. It couldn't have been written without the support and encouragement of many people in many ways.

One person has been present from sharing the very first, very tentative thoughts about writing of my experiences following Ruth's murder. My dear friend Nancy Kohner has given me the benefit of her own considerable experience as a writer. This alone would have been of great benefit, but Nancy has done far more. Throughout the years of thinking, drafting, redrafting, restructuring and preparation for publication we have met several times each year, and exchanged many phone calls, letters and e-mails. Her perceptive and challenging comments on the many drafts and redrafts have always been stimulating and encouraging. Her constancy throughout the whole process has been unfailing and I am certain the book would never have been completed without her wise counsel.

Of course, Nancy and I discussed acknowledgements in books. We agreed that we both found that quite apart from being a welcome opportunity to thank the people who helped to bring a book into being, the acknowledgements had an added interest in that they gave an insight into the way the book had developed. We also agreed that it is a daunting task, because it is impossible to name everyone who has helped or been involved, and finding the right words to express gratitude is problematical in not wanting to be bland or terse.

For well over twenty years, I have been a member of a correspondence magazine. Each member writes a letter every month. The letters are sent to the editor, who puts them in a folder that is then circulated. *Athena* is always a pleasure; I can never resist reading it as soon as it arrives. We have shared our lives and our many joys and sorrows, finding solace in each other's letters. I would like to thank Hilary Adams, Sarah Akhtar, Caroline Comer, Gillian Gatehouse, Sue Gotley, Mary Ibbotson, Matilda Popper (editor), Marina Reed and Jacqueline Taylor for responding so tenderly to my immediate anguish and longer-term low periods following Ruth's death. Since the introduction of word processors, most of us keep copies of our own letters and these have been an invaluable resource.

At a crucial stage in the first draft, I was introduced through a friend to Hannah Griffiths, who at that time was running her own agency offering advice to writers on how to structure material into a readable manuscript. We had three meetings and she injected clarity and practical wisdom on the task of writing and boosted my energy to keep going. Hannah is now a literary agent at Curtis Brown.

Another introduction by another friend led me to my agent Mandy Little of Watson, Little. She read through the first, far too long, draft over her Christmas break. Without ever making promises that the book would get into print, she has been firm and energetic both in getting the manuscript into a publishable form and in succeeding in getting interest from publishers. She and her colleagues have kept me in touch with all the developments, including the excitement of the 'auction' between publishers. My friend had advised me that Mandy 'doesn't waste her or other people's time'.

Although Mandy shifts an amazing amount of work, she also manages to share her wicked sense of humour and found the time to accompany a very nervous author to the first meeting with the publisher.

Having cut the first draft to half its original length, I sent copies to a number of people for their comments. They are: Hazel Bell (who also copy-edited the manuscript that was sent to publishers), Mike Bieber, Julia Braggins, Fran Broady, Duncan Campbell, Leon Conrad, Mary Ibbotson, Roma Iskander, Deborah Jaffé, Nancy Kohner, Marian Liebmann, Geoff Parratt, Keith Smith, Carole Tibballs, and Terry Veitch. As they come from a wide variety of backgrounds, they had different things to say and many insightful and practical comments to offer. 'So many cups of tea,' one said. There aren't as many in the final version.

When I heard that Aurum Press was the successful 'bidder' and would publish the book, Mandy said, 'They are an old-fashioned publisher in the best sense of that phrase, as they treat their authors as real people and with sensitivity.' She was absolutely right and I have enjoyed all the contact with Karen Ings, my patient and meticulous editor, and her colleagues.

I would like to thank Peter Dyer for his sensitive response to the jacket-design brief and for taking such good care of the lock of Ruth's hair. Ken Wilson designed the layout and chose the typography for the text. He achieved what I was hoping for: the pages look crisp and there is 'air' around the words. My Cornish heart was delighted to see that the book was being printed and bound in Cornwall by MPG Books of Bodmin.

Personal friends of mine, and of Ruth, and family members have been supportive and encouraging in various ways. I would like to thank my nieces Teresa and Nicola for writing down their experiences of attending the trial. My sister-in-law,

Pat Cooper, has always given me comfort despite her own great sorrow at Ruth's death.

And what of Vic, Ruth's father and my husband, and of Catherine, Ruth's sister and Vic's and my elder daughter; what has been their involvement? Neither of them has read the book as yet, and perhaps they never will. They are both very private people and would not have chosen to bring the aftermath of Ruth's death into the public arena. They have not wanted to discuss the content of the book but they have helped in lots of practical ways – for example, in ferrying boxes of paper, loaning a laser printer – and they have helped me most of all by never asking me not to write. I know that this has placed very difficult demands on them, not least when I was reliving harrowing experiences and the effort to write about them drained me.

I would like to thank all the people who appear in the book, nearly all of whom appear under their own names. A few asked for their names to be changed and this has been done. Micheal's name is his real name, and yes, that is how he spells Micheal. The name of the man who killed Ruth is not Andrew Steel. I don't want him to be traced and identified. He is serving a long prison sentence and is entitled to his privacy.

Further reading

BEREAVEMENT

The Bereaved Parents' Survival Guide
  Juliet Cassuto Rothman
  Continuum, 1997

*Coming Back: Rebuilding Lives
After Crisis and Loss*
  Ann Kaiser Stearns
  Methuen, 1989

A Grief Observed
  C. S. Lewis
  Faber Paperbacks, 1978

Necessary Losses
  Judith Viorst
  Simon & Schuster, 1988

*All In The End Is Harvest:
An Anthology for those who Grieve*
  Ed. Agnes Whitaker
  Darton, Longman & Todd in
  association with Cruse

*When Bad Things Happen
to Good People*
  Harold S. Kushner
  Pan, 1982

Man's Search for Meaning
  Viktor E. Frankl
  Hodder & Stoughton, 1987

RESTORATIVE JUSTICE

*Justice for Victims and Offenders:
A Restorative Justice Response to Crime*
  Martin Wright
  Waterside Press, 1996

*Forgiving Justice: A Quaker vision
for criminal justice*
  Tim Newell
  Quaker Home Service, 2000

DEATH PENALTY

Welcome to Hell
  Jan Arriens
  Northeastern University Press,
  Boston, 2000

*Dead Man Walking: An Eyewitness
Account of the Death Penalty in the
United States*
  Sister Helen Prejean
  Vintage, 1994

*Shot in the Heart: One Family's
History in Murder*
  Mikal Gilmore
  Penguin, 1994

MURDER

Violence: Reflections on
a National Epidemic
James Gilligan, M.D.
Vintage, 1996

Murderers and Life Imprisonment:
Containment, Treatment, Safety
and Risk
Eric Cullen and Tim Newell
Waterside Press, 1999

Life after Life:
Interviews with Twelve Murderers
Tony Parker
Secker & Warburg, 1990

In Search of the Rainbow's End:
The Inside Story of the Bamber Murders
Colin Caffell
Hodder & Stoughton, 1994

As If
Blake Morrison
Granta, 1997

Cries Unheard:
The Story of Mary Bell
Gitta Sereny
Macmillan, 1998

Victim Support
Families of Murder Victims,
Final Report, April 1990
Available on request to the
Resources Officer at the
Victim Support National
Office – see organisations list.
A small fee for the cost of
the report and postage will
be charged.

Recorded Crime Statistics,
England and Wales
Available free from
the Home Office
RDS Communications
Development Unit
Room 201
50 Queen Anne's Gate
London SW1H 9AT
And on the website:
www.homeoffice.gov.uk/rds/
hosbpubs1.html

Useful organisations

CENTRE FOR CRIME
AND JUSTICE STUDIES
King's College London
75–79 York Road
London SE1 7AW
Tel: 020 7401 2425
Fax: 020 7401 2436
E-mail: ccjs.enq@
kcl.ac.uk
www.kcl.ac.uk/ccjs

HOME OFFICE
50 Queen Anne's Gate
London SW1H 9AT
Tel: 020 7273 4599
Fax: 020 7273 2560
E-mail:
public.enquiries@
homeoffice.gsi.gov.uk
www.homeoffice.gov.uk

LAW SOCIETY
113 Chancery Lane
London WC2A 1PL
Tel: 020 7242 1222
Fax: 020 7831 0344

LIFELINES
The Well House
Furneux Pelham
Hertfordshire
SG9 OLN
www.lifelines.org

MEDIATION UK
Alexander House
Telephone Avenue
Bristol BS1 4BS
Tel: 0117 904 6661
Fax: 0117 904 3331
E-mail: enquiry@
mediationuk.org.uk
www.mediationuk.org.uk

MURDER VICTIMS' FAMILIES
FOR RECONCILIATION
2161 Massachusetts Avenue
Cambridge MA 02140, U.S.A.
Tel: 001 617 868 0007
Fax: 001 617 354 2832

(NACRO) NATIONAL
ASSOCIATION FOR THE
CARE AND RESETTLEMENT
OF OFFENDERS
169 Clapham Road
London SW9 0PU
Telephone: 020 7582 6500
Help Line: 020 7840 6464
(Mon–Fri 9 a.m.–5 p.m.)
Fax: 020 7735 4666
E-mail: communications@
nacro.org.uk
www.nacro.org.uk

THE NO WAY TRUST
H.M. Prison
Hedon Road
Hull HU9 5LS
Tel: 01482 224382
Fax: 01482 221971
E-mail: prison@
pmnw.karoo.co.uk
www.pmnw.co.uk

RELIGIOUS SOCIETY OF FRIENDS
(QUAKERS)
Friends House
173 Euston Road
London NW1 2BJ
Tel: 020 7663 1000
Fax: 020 7663 1001
E-mail: addresses on website
www.quaker.org.uk

RESTORATIVE JUSTICE
CONSORTIUM
Room 9
Winchester House
11 Cranmer Road
London SW9 6EJ
Tel: 0207 735 6592

SUPPORT AFTER MURDER
AND MANSLAUGHTER (SAMM)
Cranmer House
39 Brixton Road
London SW9 6DZ
Tel: 020 7735 3838
Helpline: 020 7735 3838
(out of office hours the help-
line is staffed by volunteers)
Fax: 020 7735 3900
E-mail: samm@ukpeople.net

VICTIM SUPPORT
Cranmer House
39 Brixton Road
London SW9 6DZ
Tel: 020 7735 9166 (admin)
Help Line: 0845 3030 900
(Mon–Fri 9 a.m.–9 p.m.,
Sat/Sun 9 a.m.–7 p.m.)
Fax: 020 7582 5712
E-mail: contact@
victimsupport.org.uk
www.victimsupport.com